Alfred Todd

A treatise on the proceedings to be adopted in conducting or opposing private bills in the Parliament of Canada; and the standing orders of both houses in relation

Fourth Edition

Alfred Todd

A treatise on the proceedings to be adopted in conducting or opposing private bills in the Parliament of Canada; and the standing orders of both houses in relation
Fourth Edition

ISBN/EAN: 9783337208110

Printed in Europe, USA, Canada, Australia, Japan

Cover: Foto ©Suzi / pixelio.de

More available books at **www.hansebooks.com**

A TREATISE

ON THE

PROCEEDINGS TO BE ADOPTED

IN CONDUCTING OR OPPOSING

PRIVATE BILLS

IN THE

Parliament of Canada;

AND THE

STANDING ORDERS OF BOTH HOUSES

IN RELATION THERETO.

BY ALFRED TODD,

CHIEF CLERK OF COMMITTEES AND PRIVATE BILLS,
HOUSE OF COMMONS.

FOURTH EDITION,

(*Prepared for the use of the Legislature of the Province of Quebec.*)

OTTAWA:

HUNTER, ROSE & COMPANY.

1869.

PREFACE.

The first Edition of this work was published in 1862, in the 1st Session of the 7th Provincial Parliament of Canada. It contained suggestions for certain changes in practice, upon which the Legislative Assembly took action in the same Session, and made such alterations in their Rules as were deemed advisable. A new Edition, embracing these changes, was, by desire of the House, prepared and and published after the close of the Session.

In the first Session of the Parliament of the Dominion, the system of Private Bill Practice that had obtained in the Provincial Legislature was adopted, with some important modifications suggested by the Hon. C. Dunkin, a Member of the House of Commons (to whom the present Edition of this work is inscribed); and a new Edition was prepared for the use of Parliament.

Upon the meeting of the Legislature of the Province of Quebec, a series of Rules in relation to Private Bills was adopted (at the instance of the same gentleman), that was substantially the same as those of the Canadian Parliament; and the Edition of this work now issued was prepared under the authority of the Legislative Assembly, for the use of the Legislature of Quebec. It is based on the latest Canadian Edition, and contains notes directing attention to the few matters of detail in which the practice of the two Legislatures differs.

OTTAWA, January, 1869.

PREFACE TO THE THIRD EDITION.

In the first Session of the first Parliament of the Dominion, the Rules and Practice in force in the old Province of Canada with regard to Private Bills were adopted by Parliament, with some modifications in the details, which, though of importance in their place, effected no material alteration in the system. These are all embodied in the present Edition of this work; and as no clearly defined Private Bill system of practice has prevailed in the Local Legislatures of Nova Scotia and New Brunswick, the precedents referred to are all taken from Canadian practice; they include those given in the last Edition, and others gleaned from subsequent legislation, both in the Provincial Parliament, and in the first Session of that of the Dominion.

In the course of the last mentioned Session, it happened upon several occasions, that doubts arose as to the true interpretation of those provisions of the "British North America Act" which placed certain classes of subjects under the exclusive control of the General Parliament, and of the Provincial Legislatures, respectively. A chapter has therefore been added, on "Legislative Jurisdiction," in which mention is made of the various questions that arose from time to time, and the course taken thereon ; and certain observations and suggestions are offered, in the hope that some plan may be devised for obtaining a more definite interpretation of the Imperial Act in this respect.

The authorities cited in explanation of the Imperial practice, are :—

Report on the practice of the House of Commons upon Private Bills: with suggestions for the future regulation of Private Business in the Legislative Assembly of Canada. By ALPHEUS TODD, Librarian to the Legislative Assembly. (1847.)

Report from a Select Committee of the House of Commons on the Business of the House. (1861.)

MAY on the Law, Privileges, Proceedings, and Usage of Parliament. Sixth edition. (1868.)

SHERWOOD on the proceedings to be adopted in conducting Private Bills through the House of Commons. Third edition. (1834.)

FRERE's Practice of Committees of the House of Commons, with reference especially to Private Bills. (1846.)

BRISTOWE on Private Bill legislation in the Imperial Parliament. (1859.)

HOUSE OF COMMONS,
    OTTAWA, November, 1868.

CONTENTS.

APPENDIX.

PROCEEDINGS

PRIVATE BILLS

THROUGH THE

PARLIAMENT OF CANADA,

[WITH NOTES APPLICABLE TO THE PRACTICE IN THE LEGISLATURE OF QUEBEC.]

~~~~~~~~~~

1.—PRELIMINARY OBSERVATIONS.

The distinction between Public and Private **Distinction between Public and Private Bills** Bills is one that has been recognized and acted upon by the Parliament of the Mother Country from a very early period, and the mode of proceeding upon the two classes of bills has also differed in some important particulars. In passing Private Bills, while Parliament still exercises its legislative functions, its proceedings also partake also of a judicial character; the parties interested in such bills appear as suitors, while those who apprehend injury are admitted as adverse parties to the suit.

Much of the formality of a Court of Justice is

maintained; conditions are required to be observed and their observance proved by the promoters of a bill, and if they abandon it and no other parties take it up, the bill is dropped, however sensible the House may be of its value.*

First provision for Private Bills in Canada.

Although this distinction was recognized by the Legislature of the old "Province of Canada" in framing Rules for its guidance at its first Session (in 1841) by the adoption of a provision requiring two months' notice of applications for private bills, and the exaction of a fee of £20 on all such bills; and also by the appointment, every Session, of a Standing Committee on Private Bills; little else was done towards the adoption of a regular system of practice until the year 1846, when the Speaker of the Legislative Assembly was authorized to cause an inquiry to be made into the system pursued in the House of Commons, with a view to the preparation of a system of Standing Orders and practice adapted to the circumstances of the Province.† The result of this was laid on the table of the House in the following Session,

Alpheus Todd's Report on Private Bill Practice.

in the shape of a Report, prepared by Mr. Alpheus Todd, the present Librarian of the Canadian House of Commons, giving a full and lucid explanation of the system of practice in operation

---

* May, p. 633.
† Assembly Journ., 1846, p. 344.

in the Imperial Parliament, and submitting a code of orders and regulations such as appeared suitable to the requirements of Canada.* No immediate action was taken upon this Report, but in the same Session the practice of referring both petitions and bills to the Committee on Private Bills indiscriminately was discontinued, and petitions were from that time referred to the Committee on Standing Orders, for proof of a compliance with the Rules of the House. In 1850, a Private Bill Office was established, in pursuance of a suggestion contained in the above-mentioned Report, and a system of practice organized, which, with some few modifications subsequently in the details, is that now in use. *Private Bill Office.*

Up to the year 1861, no regulations had been made by the Legislative Council of Canada concerning private bills, except to require an official report to the Speaker of the notices given on petitions, and the payment of a fee on all such bills as originated in that House : but in the Session of 1861, a conference was held between the two Houses, which led to the adoption, by the Council, of the Private Bill Rules of the Assembly *verbatim et literatim*.† These Rules were slightly modified in succeeding Sessions. and, in *Former practice in L. Council.*

---

* Assembly Journ., 1847, p. 31. (App. B.)
† L. Council Journ., 1861, pp. 98, 104.

the first Session of the Parliament of Canada held
Practice in both Houses now nearly identical. under the authority of the "British North America Act, 1867," they were adopted by both Houses, with some further modifications as regards the Commons, which were not made in the Rules of the Senate ; the Rules as adopted by each House, will be found at the end of this work, (Appendix I,) together with certain additional Rules of the Senate relating to Divorce Bills. (Appendix II.)*

The practice of the two Houses being thus made almost identical, the account given in the following pages, of the proceedings on Petitions and Bills in the Lower House, will apply substantially to the Upper, any diversity of practice between the two Houses being specially pointed out in the appropriate place. It should be stated, however, that the fee is charged only in the House in which the bill originates,† and all expenses for printing and translation being exacted at the same time, no payment is required to be made in the other House, except in cases where a bill is ordered to be reprinted, when the expense must be borne **In which** by its promoters. As a general rule, private bills

---

* The Rules of the Legislative Assembly of Quebec correspond with those of the House of Commons, hereto appended, and are similarly numbered : the Rules of the Legislative Council of Quebec correspond with those of the Senate (omitting the Rules relative to Divorce Bills),—but they are numbered from 47 to 70,—while the Senate Rules are numbered from 49 to 72. Some slight variations occur in regard to the printing of bills, which are referred to in the proper place.

† 58th Rule.

may originate in either House, but it being the exclusive right of the Commons to impose and appropriate all charges imposed upon the people, every bill which involves any tax, rate, toll, or duty, ought to be first brought into that House.* It has followed from this restriction that by far the greater number of private bills have been first passed by the Lower House.† It may be worthy of consideration whether it might not be desirable, in this country, also to include bills relating to Banking in this category, as they are necessarily subject to the supervision of the Minister of Finance, who has always a seat in the Commons. The Lords have generally originated naturalization, name, estate, and divorce bills,‡ but this has not been the practice with the Upper House, in this country, save only as regards divorce bills, which have invariably been introduced first into that House.

The House of Commons of Great Britain, by a Standing Order of 1858 (No. 67), have provided

House Private Bills may originate.

Arrangement between the

---

* May, pp. 437, 635.

† The House of Commons of Great Britain, by a Standing Order of 27th July, 1858, have agreed " that this House will not insist on its privileges with regard to any clauses in private bills sent down from the House of Lords, which refer to tolls and charges for services performed, and are not in the nature of a tax."

‡ May, p. 636.

twoHouses for originating bills. that the Chairman of Ways and Means, shall, at the commencement of each Session, confer with the Chairman of Committees of the House of Lords, for the purpose of determining in which House the respective private bills should be first considered, and report the same to the House.* This arrangement was the result of a recommendation contained in the 3rd Report of the Select Committee of the House of Commons on Private Bills, in 1847. (p. 6.)

---

* Bristowe's Private Bill Practice, pp. 15, 73. An example of the result of this arrangement will be seen by referring to the Commons Journals of 1860, p. 16.

2.—DEFINITION OF A PRIVATE BILL.

Every bill for the particular interest or benefit Distinction of any person or persons, is treated as a private between bill, whether it be for the interest of an individual, Private Bills. a public company or corporation, a parish, a city, a county, or other locality;* it is equally distinguished from a measure of public policy in which the whole community are interested, and this distinction is marked by the solicitation of private bills by the parties whose interests are concerned.†

There is a class of bills, however, which, though Semi-local or special in their operation, yet having been private bills. solicited by persons not in the interest of the parties to be affected by their operation, or having been introduced upon public grounds, have been treated by the Legislature as public bills. Bills of this class have occasionally been introduced as private, and referred to the Standing Committee

---

* A bill for the benefit of three Counties has been held by the British House of Commons to be a private bill. 1 Commons Journ., p. 388.

† May, p. 626.

on Private Bills, but upon their report that they were public, rather than private in their character, they have been referred by the House to another committee, and treated otherwise as public bills.* It must be obvious, however, that on bills of this nature, the same notice should be required as upon a private bill, with the exception only of such as are introduced upon some well-defined principle of public policy or right.

In 1858, the Committee on Private Bills reported, with reference to a bill to attach certain newly surveyed townships to the County of Victoria, that they were in doubt whether the bill came within their province, inasmuch as it affected the Territorial Divisions of the Province, the Representation, and the administration of Justice ; but they prepared such amendments as appeared to them desirable, and left it to the House to consider whether action should be taken on their report or not. The House took the bill into consideration with the proposed amendments, and treated it therefore as a private bill.† In 1864, the same course was taken (with a like result) in

Victoria New Townships Bill. (L. Assembly.)

---

* Quebec Recorder's Court, 1856 ; Montreal Trinity House (amending the provisions concerning pilotage), 1857 ; Quebec Harbour (a Government Trust), 1858 ; River Welland Bridges Protection, 1859 ; Caisse d'Economie de St. Roch Investigation, 1861 ; Rimouski and Gaspé division, 1865.

† Assembly Journ., 1858, pp. 568, 684.

reference to a bill respecting the Common of the Common of Lorette Indians Bill. (do.) Huron Indians at Lorette, which was not considered private, the Indians being under the special protection of the Crown.*

In the British House of Commons, may be instanced the Passing Tolls on Shipping Bill (introduced in 1856), which was held to be a public bill. Passing Tolls on Shipping Bill. (Commons). It concerned the harbours of Dover, Ramsgate, Whitby and Bridlington, abolished passing tolls, transferred the control of those harbours to the Board of Trade, imposed tolls, and repealed local Acts; but, being a measure of general policy, its character was not changed by the fact that these harbours only came under its operation. The Red Sea and India Telegraph Bill (in 1861), which amended a private Act, was introduced and passed as a public bill, as it concerned the Red Sea and India Telegraph Bill. (do.) conditions of a government guarantee.† The practice in Canada has been to treat all bills relating to the Representation,‡ the administration of Justice,§ or the protection of the Indians

---

* Assembly Journ., 1864, pp. 391, 478.

† May, p. 629.

‡ Armagh Representation, 1858; Peel do., 1858; Drummond and Arthabaska do., 1858; Bill to transfer Delaware from the West to the East Riding (Electoral Division) of Middlesex, 1862; Hochelaga polls, 1863 (Aug. Sess.)

§ Montreal Recorder's Court, 1852-3; Gaspé Circuit Court, 1852-3; Huntingdon Circuit Court, 1854-5; Montmagny do.,

and their lands and property,* however local or

Certain bills treated as public bills.
partial in their operation, as public bills, these questions being under the especial charge of the Administration, and being dealt with on broad general principles. All bills relating to Government Trusts or Commissions,† or public works under Government control,‡ are likewise so treated.

Bills introduced irregularly
Some bills, though strictly private, having been introduced irregularly (*i. e.*, not based upon petition, in the usual way), the committee have declined to proceed upon them.§ In 1864,

Rectorial lands sale Bill.
a bill to enable the Church Societies and Incorporated Synods of the Church of England Dioceses in Canada to sell the Rectorial lands in the said Dioceses, having been sent down by the Legislative Council, objection was taken at the second reading, that the bill was a private one, and should have been brought in on a petition; and

---

1858; Kamouraska Gaol and Court House, 1863 (Aug. Sess.); Quebec Recorder's Court, 1864 and 1865. See also May, p. 629.

* Common of Lorette Indians, 1864.

† Montreal Trinity House, 1857; Quebec Harbour, 1858, 1863, and 1867-8; Montreal Turnpike Road Trust, 1861; Montreal Port Warden, 1862 and 1863 (Feb. Sess.); Montreal Harbour, 1865.

‡ Northern Railway, 1859; Intercolonial Railway, 1867-8. See May, p. 662.

§ Rimouski and Gaspé division, 1865 (Jan. Sess.); Quebec Corporation, 1866.

the objection being sustained, the bill was not
proceeded with.* In 1866, objection was taken, Perth Debt
at the second reading, to a bill to extend the time Bill.
for paying the debt of the County of Perth (due
to the Municipal Loan Fund) that it, though a
private bill, affected the public revenue, and
should therefore have originated in committee of
the whole; and the objection was fatal to the
bill.† It has been held that a bill commenced
as a private bill cannot be taken up and proceeded
with as a public bill.‡

The proceedings observed in the Imperial Par- Difference
liament in the passage of private bills, are neces- between
Imperial
sarily somewhat complicated in their character, and Canadian prac-
in consequence of the numerous checks imposed tice.
for the protection of the many interests which
they may affect or involve; and the expense attending these proceedings is considerable : but
the different circumstances of this country, as one
but newly settled, allowing a freer scope for en-
terprise, with comparatively little risk of infring-
ing upon existing rights or privileges, admit (for
a time at least) of a much simpler and more inex-
pensive system of Private Bill legislation. In explaining the system adopted (after various modi-

---

* Assembly Journ., 1865 (Aug. Sess.), p. 123.
† Assembly Journ., 1866, p. 293.
‡ May, p. 631.

Proceed-
ings in
Commons
to be des-
cribed first.

fications) by our Legislature, it is proposed to state the various forms and proceedings so far as can conveniently be done, in the order in which they occur, from the presentation of the petition (in either House) to the final passage of the bill. It will be convenient for this purpose to begin with the House of Commons, but the course observed in either House being now identical (with the exception of proceedings upon Divorce Bills in the Upper House, which are described in the latter part of this work, and certain matters of detail with reference to private bills generally, which are noticed in the proper place), the description will apply equally to bills originating in the Senate.

3.—LEGISLATIVE JURISDICTION

REGARDING PRIVATE BILLS.

By the provisions of "The British North America Act, 1867," certain classes of Private Bills are placed under the exclusive control of the Parliament of the Dominion, and certain others are transferred to the Provincial Legislatures.

The classes of subjects which, under this arrangement, pertain exclusively to the *Parliament of the Dominion*, are thus defined by the Act : *Subjects under control of Parliament.*

Sec. 91.—Ferries between a Province and any British or Foreign Country, or between two Provinces.

Banking, Incorporation of Banks, and the issue of Paper Money.

Savings Banks.

Patents of Invention and Discovery.

Naturalization and Aliens.

Marriage and Divorce,—and

Such classes of subjects as are expressly excepted

2

Subjects
under
control of
Parlia-
ment.
in the enumeration of the classes of subjects
by this Act assigned exclusively to the
Legislatures of the Provinces ; which exceptions are thus defined, in

Sec. 92, Sub-section 10:

a. Lines of Steam or other Ships, Railways,
Canals, Telegraphs, and other Works and
Undertakings connecting the Province
with any other or others of the Provinces,
or extending beyond the limits of the
Province :

b. Lines of Steam Ships between the Province
and any British or Foreign Country :

c. Such Works as, although wholly situate
within the Province, are before or after
their execution declared by the Parliament
of Canada to be for the general advantage
of Canada, or for the advantage of two or
more of the Provinces.

Subjects
under con-
trol of Pro-
vincial
Legisla-
tures.
Those which are placed under the exclusive
control of the *Provincial Legislatures* are thus
defined :

Sec. 92, Sub-sec. 10.—Local Works and Undertakings, other than such as form the exceptions above recited.

Sub-sec. 11.—The incorporation of Companies
with Provincial objects.

Sub-sec. 16.—Generally all matters of a merely local or private nature in the Province.

It will be observed that the line of distinction is defined clearly with regard to certain classes of subjects only. Sub-section 10 empowers the Parliament of Canada to assume the control of any works wholly situate within one Province, that may be declared by that Body to be for the advantage of the Dominion, or of two or more Provinces. Two instances of this occurred in the first Session of Parliament, in the case of the Bill to incorporate the proprietors of the Ottawa and Prescott Railway, by the name of "The St. Lawrence and Ottawa Railway Company," and the Bill respecting the Northern Railway of Canada—in the enactment of each of which bills, Parliament declared that the Railway therein referred to was "a work for the general advantage of Canada."* The first mentioned bill contained a provision empowering the St. Lawrence and Ottawa Railway Company to build a bridge over the River Ottawa, and to construct a branch to Lake Deschesnes, in the Province of Quebec; but it was argued, in debate, that this would not in itself justify legislation by the Parliament of Canada, in reference to a Railway situate wholly within one Province, as it might afford a dangerous precedent to parties desirous of evading the jurisdiction of the Local Legislatures over works of a purely local character; and the course was

Marginal notes: Works declared to be for the general advantage. St. Lawrence & Ottawa Railway. Northern Railway.

---

* 31 Vic., c. 20, sec. 1, and c. 86, sec. 2.

adopted of introducing the clause above mentioned, in order to bring the bill properly within the jurisdiction of the Parliament of the Dominion.

All Railways intersecting Grand Trunk should be under same control. These Railways are, thus far, the only ones of a local character that have been legislated upon by Parliament; but an impression would appear to prevail, that all Railways intersecting the Grand Trunk should be under the same Parliamentary control, to avoid the serious difficulties and inconveniences that might arise (so long as they are subject to a different jurisdiction) from conflicting regulations in reference to the running of trains, inspection of Railway, gauge, and other matters of detail.

Works extending beyond limits of a Province. There is a class of Railways and other works included among those placed by section 92 (sub-sec. 10, *a*), under the exclusive control of the Parliament of the Dominion, that is referred to with some little ambiguity. The section reads " Lines of Steam or other ships, Railways, &c., connecting the Province with any other or others of the Provinces, *or extending beyond the limits of the Province.*" It is clear that the words " extending beyond the limits of the Province" cannot have been intended to apply to works merely connecting two adjacent Provinces, because they are described in the words immediately preceding. Nor, on the other hand, can they refer to any Railway or other work actually extending into a foreign country, because, in the very nature of things, no such power of extension can be conferred by Canadian legislation. It would appear therefore that these words must have reference to such Railways, Telegraphs, or other works, as lead directly into a foreign country, such, for example, as the Great Western Railway, which connects directly with the United States Railway system, both at the Niagara Falls Suspension Bridge, and also at Detroit,—the Buffalo and Lake Huron Railway, connecting with United States Railways at Buffalo,—the Montreal and Champlain Railway, connecting at Rouse's Point with the Vermont Central, &c.

Several bills were passed by Parliament, in the Session of 1867-8, relating to works of this class, *viz.* :—To amend the Act for the incorporation of the North-west Navigation and Railway Co. (a Company empowered, among other things, to navigate Lakes Huron and Superior within the limits of Canada),—To confirm a By-law passed by the Directors of the Lake Memphremagog Navigation Company (whose steamers ply on a lake partly within the territory of the United States),—To incorporate the Clifton Suspension Bridge Co. (international),—and to authorize the carrying of gas pipes across the River Niagara, in order to facilitate the lighting of the Town of

Works of this class legislated on in 1867-8.

---

* It should be mentioned, however, that the Quebec Legislature, at their first Session, passed an Act to amend the Act incorporating the Massawippi Valley Railway Co. (31 Vic., c. 45),—and the Ontario Legislature passed an Act for the incorporation of the Erie and Niagara Extension Railway Co. (31 Vic., c. 14.) Both of these Railways are of the class here referred to, and as their operation was not interfered with by the Dominion Government, it must be assumed that the Provincial Legislatures, in enacting them, were not considered to have exceeded their jurisdiction.

Clifton with gas (international). As none of these bills contained the "general advantage" clause, it may be assumed that the construction put by Parliament upon the provisions of the Imperial Act in regard to bills of this class agrees with that above suggested.

Companies for doing business throughout the Dominion. There is another class of bills, concerning which serious doubts have arisen in regard to jurisdiction, namely, those for the incorporation of companies for the transaction of business of any kind *throughout the Dominion.* Sub-section 11 (above quoted) assigns to the Provincial Legislatures "the incorporation of companies with Provincial objects." In the first Session of the Parliament of the Dominion, several petitions were presented in reference to the incorporation, &c., of Insurance and other private companies. Upon two of these, praying respectively for the incorporation of the Gore District Mutual Fire Insurance Company, and of the Sorghum Growers' Association of the County of Essex, the Committee on Standing Orders (Commons) reported, in each case, that in their opinion the matter " came more properly within the jurisdiction of the Local Legislature of Ontario."* On the other hand, petitions for the incorporation of

---

* 5th and 8th Reports of Committee on Standing Orders (Commons), 1867-8.

the Merchants' Express Company of the Dominion of Canada,—for the incorporation of the Canadian Lake Underwriters' Association,—and for amending the Acts relating to the Canada West Farmers' Mutual and Stock Insurance Company, and changing the name to the Canada Farmers' Mutual Insurance Company, were reported upon favorably, and bills, introduced upon them, were passed, and became law.*   Another petition, for an Act to grant certain powers to the Civil Service Building and Savings Society, was reported on favorably by the Standing Orders Committee of each House, and a bill introduced in the Commons.   This bill was subsequently referred to the Committee on Banking and Commerce, who, after discussing, in committee, the question of jurisdiction, presented a report to the House, representing that "doubts had arisen as to whether the objects sought to be obtained by the promoters were not Provincial in their character, and such as the Local Legislature is exclusively empowered to deal with,"† and soliciting instruction on the subject.   A similar proceeding took place on the part of the Private Bill Committee of the Senate, who presented a

---

* 31 Vic., chaps. 90, 91 and 93.

† 5th Report of Committee on Banking and Commerce (Commons), 1867-8.

report of a like nature in reference to a Bill to incorporate the Intercolonial Insurance Company.* A discussion ensued upon the Report, which resulted in the appointment of a committee " to inquire into and report to this House on the classes of Acts for the incorporation of private companies, which properly, under the ' British North America Act, 1867,' come within the jurisdiction of the Parliament of the Dominion, and to act on behalf of this House as Members of any Joint Committee of the Senate and House of Commons, which may be ordered on the subject." † No committee was appointed on the part of the Commons, and no further steps were taken with regard to either of the above mentioned bills.

Inquiry into question of jurisdiction.

It was urged, on the part of the promoters of these bills, that the companies to which they related were desirous of transacting business in different parts of the Dominion, and were therefore in need of more extensive and general powers than could be conferred upon them by a Provincial Legislature, and, in short, that they were not properly of the class referred to in Subsection 11 of the Act, as "Companies with Provincial objects." Against this it was argued that

Status of Provincial corporations.

---

* Report of Committee on Standing Orders and Private Bills (Senate), 5th Dec., 1867.

† Senate Journal, 12th Dec., 1867.

a Provincial Charter would suffice to ensure their recognition in every Province where their Agencies might be established ; and that under such a charter they could sue and be sued, and transact all business of an ordinary character. In opposition to this view, a case was cited by the Honorable Mr. Campbell, in the debate in the Senate on the Bill to incorporate the Intercolonial Insurance Company, having an immediate bearing upon the question as to the *status* in one Province of a company incorporated by the Legislature of another Province. The case referred to was an action brought, in the Court of King's Bench of Upper Canada, by the Bank of Montreal, in the year 1836 (prior to the Union of Upper and Lower Canada), for the recovery of the amount of certain promissory notes, the drawers and endorsers of which resided in Upper Canada. The Court ruled that "a foreign corporation, such as a Bank, cannot maintain an action upon promissory notes received and discounted by them in the course of banking business in this Province, although they may maintain an action for money had and received to their use, against the person for whom such notes were discounted, and to whom money was advanced upon them."*

Case of Montreal Bank *vs.* Bethune, 1836.

---

* Bank of Montreal *vs.* Bethune, Hilary Term, 6 Wm. 4. (See Robinson & Harrison's Digest, p. 128.)

By this decision it would appear, that whatever *status* a company, owing its existence to a Provincial Charter, may possess beyond the limits of its own Province, there are limitations and restrictions which can only be obviated by special legislation in each Province. Banking Companies are, by the Act, placed under the exclusive control of the Parliament of the Dominion, and it may be found advisable, with a view of meeting the difficulty, that all commercial companies doing business of such a nature as to require the establishment of agencies in the different Provinces of the Dominion, should be placed under the same jurisdiction.

Foreign corporations in England and United States.

Angell & Ames, in their " Treatise on the Law of Private Corporations aggregate," (6th edition, Boston, 1858.) state (in treating on the powers of foreign corporations, s. 372), that " a company, claiming to be incorporated, has only to shew that it has been regularly and effectually made a corporate body, to enable it to sustain a suit beyond the jurisdiction within which it is constituted." They cite the case of the Dutch West India Company,—that of the National Bank of St. Charles, in Spain, and other analogous cases, in which it was decided by the English Courts, that a foreign corporation may maintain a suit in England by their corporate name. In the United States also, it is shewn (s. 373), that the power of a corporation to sue, in the respective States, is not restricted to companies created by the laws of the State in which the suit is instituted, but may be exercised by foreign corporations, belonging either to another State of the Confederacy, or to a foreign country. It is, however, admitted that this power is exercised rather upon sufferance than of right, as " the Legislature undoubtedly has power to prohibit foreign corporations (*i. e.*, those not created by the laws of the State) from contracting in the State ; but until it does so, contracts so made will be enforced." (s. 374.) But instances are given in which the powers of foreign corporations were restricted by the Courts without such Legislative intervention. In Virginia the Court ruled (in *re* Bank of Marietta *vs.* Pindall), that " though, as a general rule, a corporation created by the laws of one State might sue in another, it would *not be permitted to a Bank in Ohio* to establish an agency in Virginia for discounting notes, or for carrying on any other banking operations; nor could they sustain an action on any note thus acquired by them," though they admitted " there was nothing in the policy of the laws of Virginia which restrained its citizens from borrowing money from a Bank in Ohio," &c. It was also held, by the Supreme Court of the State of New York, " that a foreign corporation, keeping an office in that State, for

Bank of Marietta in Virginia.

Decision of Supreme Court of New York.

receiving deposits and discounting notes, without being expressly authorized by the laws of that State to do so, *cannot maintain an action* for the money loaned."

Difference between Constitutions of Canada and United States. These, it is true, are but rare and exceptional cases, yet they (with that relating to the Montreal Bank, before referred to), serve to shew that the powers of a corporation, beyond the territorial jurisdiction of the legislature creating it, are, in fact, exercised by permission rather than right, and are therefore subject to restriction or curtailment at any time. In considering what may be the true position of corporations created in this country under Provincial authority, it is well to bear in mind the very important difference that exists between the Constitution of the Dominion of Canada and that of the United States in regard to " State rights :" while, in the latter, the sovereignty of each State, in all matters of internal policy, is distinctly recognized and admitted, and all rights not expressly assigned by the constitution to the Federal Government are exercised by the Sovereign State,—under the constitution of Canada, the Sovereignty is expressly vested in the Government and Parliament of the Dominion, who have exclusive control over all matters not assigned exclusively to the Legislatures of the Provinces (British North America Act, sec. 91, class 29). This can hardly fail to have some effect upon the *status* of Corporations holding Provincial Charters, in any transactions they may have beyond the limits of their own Province. The Legislature of Ontario, at their first Session, in incorporating the Royal Canadian Insurance Company, expressly restricted their operations to risks "within the Province of Ontario." Insurance business, like that of Banks, is not confined to a particular locality, but is necessarily spread over the country, and the larger companies would probably desire to extend their operations over the greater part of the Dominion, and even beyond it (as regards Marine Insurance); it is therefore of importance to them that their corporate powers should proceed from the highest legislative authority in the land. An Act respecting Insurance Companies,* passed in the first Session of the Parliament of Canada, requires all such companies to obtain a licence from the Minister of Finance, and to invest a large proportion of their paid-up capital in Dominion Stock, and contains other provisions

Royal Canadian Insur. Co. (Ontario).

Insurance Companies.

---

* At one stage of this bill an objection was made, that it was beyond the jurisdiction of the House, which was over-ruled by Mr. Speaker; at another stage, a motion "that the regulation of Insurance Companies is a subject properly within the jurisdiction of the Provincial Legislatures," was proposed and negatived. (Com. Journal, 1867–8, pp. 161, 426.) It is but fair to remark, however, that this motion having been offered for the purpose of defeating the bill, and not as a substantive proposition, its bearing upon the question of jurisdiction is not so conclusive as if it had been discussed exclusively upon its own merits.

3

for securing the proper management of the companies. This affords an additional reason why it is desirable that Insurance Companies should be created by the same authority that exercises over them such stringent control.

In the first Session of the Legislature of Ontario, an Act was passed to incorporate the Guelph Board of Trade. In the first Session of the Parliament of the Dominion, a bill was introduced to incorporate the Stratford Board of Trade; the bill was referred to the Committee on Banking and Commerce, and the question of jurisdiction being raised in committee, the committee came to the conclusion that though the Board to be created was a local Board, the terms of the 91st section of the "British America Act," in placing "the Regulation of Trade and Commerce" under the control of Parliament, justified the action of this Legislature in the matter. In examining the details of the bill, however, it was found to contain provisions for the establishment of a Court of Arbitration in commercial matters; and as "the constitution, maintenance, and organization of Provincial Courts, both of civil and criminal jurisdiction," are, by the 92nd section of the said Act assigned exclusively to the Provincial Legislatures, the committee expunged from the bill so much as related to a Court of Arbitration, and it was passed in the amended form.

It is much to be desired that steps should be

Boards of Trade.

taken without delay to determine more accurately the question of jurisdiction, either by the action of the Canadian Parliament, or, if that be deemed insufficient, by invoking the interposition of the Imperial Parliament, to pass an explanatory Act.

As a preliminary step, it might be advisable to appoint a committee (upon which the various interests, Provincial and Dominional, should be duly represented), for the purpose of carefully considering the whole question of jurisdiction, and suggesting such amendments to the British America Act as may be found desirable, in order to determine doubtful points. Upon their report, an address to the Crown could be voted, soliciting the passage of an explanatory Act by the Imperial Parliament.

Another mode of meeting the difficulty has been suggested, *viz.* : that each bill upon which a doubt as to jurisdiction might be raised, should be discussed, and the point decided upon its own merits ; and that in this manner a series of precedents would be established for future guidance. Not to mention other objections that might exist to this course, there is one that cannot be overlooked, *viz.*, that the legislation of the Dominion Parliament cannot legally over-ride or interfere with the rights and privileges of the Provincial Legislatures, save in certain exceptional matters, as public works, and education ; such powers as are vested in the Local Legislatures being (with these exceptions) *exclusively* assigned to them, any proceeding or decision of Parliament upon a matter in any way exceeding its jurisdiction, instead of forming a precedent, would, in all probability, lead to the interposition of the Courts, and perhaps involve endless litigation. It is therefore of the utmost importance, that any attempt that may be made to deal with the question of jurisdiction, should be undertaken with due caution and deliberation.

4.—PARLIAMENTARY AGENTS.

In the Imperial Parliament, every private bill or petition must be solicited by a Parliamentary Agent, who conducts the bill through its various stages, and is personally responsible to the House and to the Speaker for the observance of the rules, orders, and practice of Parliament, and for the payment of all fees and charges : and no proceeding upon any petition or bill can take place, until an appearance to act as the Parliamentary Agent upon the same shall have been entered in the Private Bill Office.* This practice of employing Parliamentary Agents has been but recently introduced in Canada, and it has not hitherto been made obligatory, though the increase of business may possibly render it desirable to adopt some such course, in order that members may be relieved from a duty that is often inconvenient and embarrassing, and frequently involves a sacrifice of time and trouble, which should not in fairness be expected of them.

Parliamentary Agents must be employed in Imp'l Parliament

Not obligatory in Canada.

---

* May, p. 655.

In the revised code of Rules prepared by the late Sir Henry Smith (then Speaker), and adopted by the Assembly of 1860, provision was made for the recognition of Parliamentary Agents, **Mode of qualifying.** who had up to that time acted in a private and irresponsible capacity. No person is now permitted to Act as Parliamentary Agent, without the express sanction and authority of the Speaker.* This having been obtained, he is required to sign a declaration before the Chief Clerk of the Private Bill Office, engaging to observe and obey all the Rules of the House, and to pay all fees and charges, when demanded, and further, to enter into a recognizance in $2,000 (if required at any future time by the Speaker) conditioned to observe such declaration. His name is then registered in a book, and he is entitled to act as a Parliamentary Agent, but is liable to an absolute or temporary prohibition to practise (at the **Disqualifi- cations.** pleasure of the Speaker), for any wilful violation of the Rules and practice of Parliament, or of any rules prescribed by the Speaker. Members†

---

* 73rd and 74th Rules, Commons.

† The House of Commons of Great Britain, by a Resolution of the 26th February, 1830, declared, *nem. con.*, "That it is contrary to the law and usage of Parliament that any Member of this House should be permitted to engage, either by himself or any partner, in the management of private bills before this or the

and Officers of the House* are alike disqualified for Parliamentary Agency.

The name and place of residence of the Parliamentary Agent soliciting a bill are entered in the Private Bill Register, in which are also recorded all the proceedings, from the petition to the passing of the bill. This book is open to public inspection.†

Registration of Agents.

The Rules relating to Parliamentary Agents belong only to the House of Commons, no regulations having been adopted by the Senate on this subject.

It is usual for the Member who presents the petition to take charge of the bill through its different stages.‡

Members in charge.

---

other House of Parliament, for a pecuniary reward." Commons Journ. (G. B.), 1830, p. 107.

One of the Sessional Orders of the Canadian House of Commons also declares "that the offer of any money or other advantage to any Member of the House of Commons, for the promoting of any matter whatsoever, depending or to be transacted in the Parliament of the Dominion of Canada, is a high crime and misdemeanor, and tends to the subversion of the Constitution. Commons Journ., 1867–8, p. 5.

* In the Imperial Parliament, in compliance with the recommendation of a Select Committee on the House of Commons Offices in 1835, no officer or clerk belonging to the establishment is allowed to transact private business before the House, for his emolument or advantage, either directly or indirectly. May, p. 656.

† 71st Rule.

‡ Sherwood on Private Bills, p. 29.

5.—PETITIONS FOR PRIVATE BILLS

Every Private Bill based on a petition.

Every private bill is based on a petition,* which should state, in general terms, the objects or privileges sought to be obtained by the parties soliciting the bill, and be signed by the parties themselves (the signatures of agents on behalf of others being inadmissable, except in case of incapacity by sickness); and at least one signature should be on the same sheet on which the petition is written.† The petition is presented by a Member in his place.‡ Petitions should be prepared in triplicate, one copy being presented in each House by a Member, and a third addressed to the Governor General in Council, through the Secretary of State. (A form of petition to each branch of the Legislature will be found in the

How presented.

---

* 56th Rule. Bills relating to local improvements are occasionally brought in, in the Imperial Parliament, by order, without a petition, but are subsequently dealt with as private bills, as regards proof of compliance with standing orders, &c. May, p. 661.

† May, p. 509.

‡ 85th Rule, Commons.

Appendix, No. III.) In 1859 a Bill to incorpo- Bills which had not been based rate the Guelph and Wellington Roads Company, on a peti- was sent down by the Legislative Council, and tion. was subsequently referred to the Committee on Private Bills, who finding that it was not founded on a petition, reported that the preamble was not proved. In 1862, a Bill to separate the township of Broughton from the County of Megantic, and to annex it to the County of Beauce, which had been introduced as a public bill (under a public title), was referred to the committee, who reported that it was not based on a petition, and could not therefore be treated as a private bill; and no further proceeding was taken on the bill by the House.

The petition must be presented within the Time of presenta- first three weeks of the Session.* It was former- tion. ly the custom to extend this time, by Resolution, to a very late period of the Session, but the injurious tendency of such an extension has become so evident, from the necessity it frequently involves of dispensing with those formalities which are so necessary for the protection of private rights, that of late years there has been evinced an increasing unwillingness to extend the period. While in 1858, it was extended to 85 days from the commencement of the Session; in 1859 and

---

* 49th Rule:

1860, it was extended to 63, and in 1861 to 36 days only; the latter being but 15 days beyond the time fixed by the Rule. In 1867-8, an adjournment from December to March having been determined upon, the time for receiving petitions was extended to three weeks after the re-assembling of Parliament, and subsequently to the end of the then current month.

After expiration of time.

When the time has actually expired, parties are at liberty to present a petition, asking leave to introduce their petition for a private bill notwithstanding such expiry, and explaining the circumstances under which they have been prevented from complying with the orders of the House.* It is competent then to the House, either to grant the requisite permission upon motion,† or, in accordance with the practice in the Imperial Parliament,‡ to refer the matter to the Standing Orders Committee, and take action upon their report. In 1866, the House extended the time in favor of a particular application only.§

---

* Niagara Harbour and Dock Co., 1851; Randall Estate, 1852-3; Brockville and Ottawa Railway, 1863 (Feb. Sess.); Ottawa and French River communication, 1863 (Aug. Sess.) See also Sherwood on Private Bills, pp. 10, 23.

† Assembly Journ., 1852-3, p. 347; 1863 (Feb. Sess.), pp. 320, 326.

‡ May, p. 669.

§ Cobourg and Peterboro' Railway, 1866.

6.--PROOF OF NOTICES,

BEFORE COMMITTEE ON STANDING ORDERS.

All petitions for private bills, when received by the House, are taken into consideration (without special reference) by the Committee on Standing Orders, whose duty it is to ascertain whether the Rule of the House in regard to the publication of notice has been complied with in each case, and to report to the House the result of their inquiries; together with any recommendation that may appear to them desirable in cases where the notice may prove in any respect informal or insufficient.* The committee has no power to inquire into the merits of any such petition, this being a duty which pertains to the Private Bill Committee in considering the preamble of the bill.†

Examination of petitions without reference.

All private bills from the Senate (not being based on a petition already so reported on) are

Private Bills from Senate examined.

---

* 53rd Rule.
† Alpheus Todd's Report on Private Bills, 1847.

taken into consideration and reported upon by the committee after the first reading.*

In 1862, the Legislative Assembly (in pursuance of a recommendation of the Standing Orders Committee in their 10th Report) appointed the Chief Clerk of the Private Bill Office their " Examiner for Standing Orders," assigning to him the duty of examining into the facts with regard to the notice given on each petition, and reporting the same for the information of the Committee on Standing Orders; and the practice is continued under the new arrangements since Confederation. The committee are then enabled, upon the evidence reported to them, to decide upon each case. This corresponds with the course taken in the Imperial Parliament;† it has been adopted, as yet, only by the Lower House, and is a step towards the assimilation of our Canadian practice to that of the two Houses of the Imperial Parliament for the joint proof of their Standing Orders.‡

Examiner for Standing Orders.

---

* 54th Rule. Toronto Boys' Home, 1861 ; Huron College, 1863 (Feb. Sess.); London and Canadian Loan and Agency Co., 1863 (Aug. Sess.) ; Niagara District Bank, 1867–8.

† Bristowe, pp. 10, 77.

‡ In 1854 the Lords adopted a most convenient arrangement which dispensed with a double proof of the Orders common to both Houses; they resolved on the appointment of examiners for Standing Orders for their Lordships' House, and appointed the

All questions arising in the committee are decided by a majority of voices; the chairman voting only when there is an equality of voices. In committees on private bills, the chairman votes as a member, and has also a second or casting vote when the votes are equal; but this power is specially conferred by a Standing Order of the House;* such is also the case in Election Committees, as regulated by statute; but as regards other committees, in the absence of any special power, it is contrary to the practice of Parliament.†

The Standing Orders Committee usually appoint certain days for sitting, in the Private Bill Office, when such petitions for private bills as have been received by the House, are laid before them. In cases where there is any doubt as to

---

same gentlemen who held the office of Examiners of petitions in the House of Commons, who were thus enabled to take the evidence on the part of both Houses simultaneously: and in cases where any of the Orders have not been complied with, the Standing Orders Committee in each House determines, upon the facts reported by them, whether the same ought or ought not to be dispensed with. "Of all the improvements," says May, "connected with Private Bill legislation, none have been so signal as those in which both Houses have concurred for the assimilation and joint proof of their standing orders." May, pp. 615, 646.

* 63rd Rule.

† May, p. 386.

4

the sufficiency of the notice, the promoters of a petition appear before the committee, to produce such evidence as they may desire to offer.

Notices required in England. While the requirements of the standing orders of the Lords and Commons, relating to private bills, involve notices in various forms, and the depositing of plans, estimates, and other documents in some cases,* those of our Canadian Legislature (see Appendix I.) embrace (in all but Divorce cases) but one form of notice, *viz.*, by advertisement inserted in the *Canada Gazette*, and In Canada. also in some newspaper published in any locality that may be affected by the proposed scheme, clearly and distinctly specifying the nature and object of the application ; if the matter relate specially to the Province of Quebec, it must be published both in English and French. This notice must be continued, not less than once a week, for a period of two months, during the interval of time between the close of the preceding Session and the consideration of the petition by the committee. In the case of a proposal to erect a toll bridge, the notice must state the rates of

---

* They are arranged in the following order :—1. Notices by advertisement. 2. Notices and applications to owners, lessees, and occupiers of lands and houses. 3. Documents required to be deposited, and the times and places of deposit. 4. Form in which plans, books of reference, sections and cross sections shall be prepared. 5. Estimates and deposit of money and declarations in certain cases. May, p. 644.

toll to be demanded, the extent of the exclusive
privilege, the height of the arches, the interval
between the abutments of piers for the passage
of rafts and vessels, and, when it is intended to
construct a draw-bridge, the dimensions of the
same.*

When the application is for a Bill of Divorce,† In Divorce
the notice is required by the Standing Orders of cases.
the Senate (see Appendix II.) to be published
during six months in the *Canada Gazette*, and in
two newspapers published in the District (in
Quebec), or County or Union of Counties (in the
other Provinces), where the applicant resides.‡
A copy of such notice in writing must also be
served on the person from whom such Divorce is
sought, if the residence of such person can be
ascertained ; and proof on oath of such service
(or of the attempts made to effect the same), must
be adduced before the Senate on the reading
of the petition.§   An exemplification of all proceedings that may have been had in any Court
of Law, duly certified, must be presented at the
same time.‖   And in all cases where damages
have been awarded to the applicant, proof on

---

* 51st and 52nd Rules.

† Divorce cases are placed under the exclusive jurisdiction of
the Parliament of Canada, by sec. 91 of the British North
America Act.

‡ 73rd Rule, Senate.

§ 74th Rule, Senate.

‖ 75th Rule, Senate.

oath must be adduced that such damages have been levied and retained, or such explanation afforded for the neglect or inability to levy the same under a writ of execution, as may appear sufficient excuse for such omission.*

The various notices required by the Rules of the two Houses having been thus referred to, it should be mentioned that they do not apply to all applications for private bills, indiscriminately, but to such only as involve the granting of exclusive rights or privileges, or a possible interference with the rights or interests of other parties.† Thus petitions for the incorporation of religious, benevolent, social, literary, or educational institutions or associations,‡ for the naturalization of aliens,§ for some individual or personal advantage not of an exclusive charac-

---

* 76th Rule, Senate.

† 51st Rule (both Houses).

‡ Toronto House of Industry, 1852–3; St. Mary's College, 1852–3; German Evangelical Church incorporation, 1854–5; Canadian Order of Odd Fellows, 1856; Woodstock Literary Institute, 1857; Montreal St. Andrew's Society, 1858; Toronto Horticultural Society, 1860; Montreal Skating Club, 1861; Toronto Savings Bank, 1861; Montreal Natural History Society, 1862; Toronto Club, 1863; Humane Society of B. N. Am., 1864; St. Catharines Hospital, 1865; London Board of Trade, 1866.

§ Chaffee's naturalization, 1857; Steckel's naturalization, 1857. In the case of De Stoeckliu's naturalization (1860), and

ter,* or for objects of a like nature, have usually been reported upon by the committee as exempt from the necessity of such notice; as have also applications for amendment of existing charters, when such amendment does not interfere with the rights of shareholders or others.†

Petitions have occasionally come before the committee, seeking certain powers or privileges, which, though not "exclusive" or directly involving (in the words of the 51st Rule) "any matter or thing which in its operation would affect the rights or property of other parties," might yet tend incidentally to affect the same. In such cases they have generally reported that notice was not required (under the terms of the Rule), but that provision should be made in the Bill for duly protecting all existing rights, &c.; ‡ it then becomes

Provision in Bill, to supply want of notice.

Rogers' do. (1866), a suspension of the Rule relative to notice was recommended; and in those of Sanford and Rogers (1862) a Gazette notice was reported as sufficient.

* Mercer's relief, 1859; Poe's change of name, 1862; Ottawa Sisters of Charity (power to mortgage their property), 1863.

† Montreal Cemetery Co., 1852–3; Niagara Bank (extension of time for paying up stock), 1857; Eastern Townships Bank (reduction of capital), 1858; Port Whitby & Lake Huron Railroad Co. (do.), 1859; Toronto Cotton Mills Co., 1862; Jacques Cartier Bank, 1863; Merchants' Bank, 1864; Hamilton Board of Trade, 1866; London do., 1867–8.

‡ Platt Estate, 1858; Montreal and Champlain Railroad amendment, 1860; Guelph debt consolidation, 1860; Montreal Bank amendment, 1861, &c.

the duty of the Committee on Private Bills (or other committee of a like character), when the bill comes before them, to see that it contains such a provision, before they report it to the House.*

In the fulfilment of their duty of examining into the notices given by the promoters of private bills in compliance with the 51st and 52nd Rules, the Committee on Standing Orders have generally been guided rather by the spirit than the letter of the requirement. In every case where the formal notice proves to have been insufficient, or to have been omitted altogether, they have admitted evidence to shew that all parties whose interests may be affected by the matter in question, have been fully informed of the intention to apply to Parliament. In admitting the propriety of such a distinction in the interpretation of the Rules, it must nevertheless be remembered that parties at a distance who may be aware of an existing informality, may be led to suppose that it will be fatal to the measure, and may therefore neglect to take any steps to oppose it, relying upon the House to carry out its own Standing Orders. This has, in fact, been the case in several instances, and a knowledge of it generally acts upon the committee in exercising their judgment as to the admissability of evidence of this kind. When the committee have become satisfied in this manner

Evidence of publicity, when no notice is given.

---

* 64th Rule.

concerning a notice thus technically defective or Informality waived, in certain cases. informal, they have in some instances taken upon themselves to waive the informality, and to report the notice as sufficient. Thus, publication of the proceedings at a public meeting called to consider a certain question, or some other public notice,* discussions in reference thereto in a City Council, reported in the local papers,† or service of notice on the shareholders of a company individually, or evidence of the knowledge or consent of parties affected,‡ have been held to be a sufficient substitute for the notice required by the Rule. They have dispensed with the local notice in a matter affecting a remote and unsettled part of the country,§ also, in the incorporation of Insurance Companies,‖ or Banks,¶ and in other

---

* Three Rivers Diocese Church Rate, 1852–3; Joliette incorporation, 1863; Bruce County Town, 1864.

† Montreal Corporation amendment, 1856; Montreal City Passenger Railway, 1861; Toronto incorporation amendment, 1862; Quebec Corporation, 1861.

‡ Hamilton Hotel Co., 1856; Upper Canada Bank, 1862; Brockville & Ottawa Railway, 1863; Woodstock Literary Institute, 1864; Ottawa & Prescott Railway, 1865; McDougall Estate, 1865; Bruce By-law, 1866; St. Lawrence Tow Boat Co., 1866; Merchants' Bank, 1867–8.

§ Huron Copper Bay Co., 1849; Sault St. Marie Canal, 1852–3.

‖ British America Fire and Life Assurance Co., 1852–3, &c.

¶ Royal Bank of Canada, 1861, &c.

matters not affecting any particular locality.* They have also dispensed with notice in the Official Gazette in applications of a purely local nature,† and with the French local notice in a matter relating to the Eastern Townships of Lower Canada,‡ and the English local notice in one affecting a population of French origin.§

Suspension of Rule relative to notice. The above cases must however be considered as altogether exceptional; while the committee may, in their discretion, interpret the Rules in the most liberal sense, they have no power to dispense with the formalities required by the House. When, after due examination, they consider it desirable to relax these formalities in any particular case, they report the facts to the House, and recommend a suspension of the Rule. The principal grounds upon which a suspension has been recommended may be thus stated:—Evidence of consent of parties interested, ‖ —That

* In companies of this nature, whose business is general rather than local, it is customary, when an amendment of their Charter is asked, to publish a local notice (in addition to that in the Official Gazette) in a newspaper circulating at the seat of their chief place of business.

† Iroquois School Section, 1858; Moulton Division, 1859; Cobourg Manufacturing Co., 1859; Burford Survey, 1860; Fitzroy Survey, 1863; Becancour Bridge, 1863; Fabriques Mutual Assurance, 1865.

‡ Iberville, Brome, Shefford, and Missisquoi Road, 1857.

§ Joliette Mining Co., 1857; Tring Municipality, 1863.

‖ Galt Estate, 1860; La Banque du People stock increase,

all parties have signed the petition,* —or are sufficiently apprized of the application,† —That the petition (in matters of a local nature) is very generally signed,‡ —That no private rights will be interfered with,§ —Proceedings in reference thereto at a public meeting,‖ or in City Councils,¶ —That the notice will have fully matured before any action can be taken on the bill by the

---

1861; Beauharnois Presbyterian Cong., 1861; Grand Trunk Railway, 1862; Dumble's relief, 1863; St. Thomas Debentures, 1864; McCallum's relief, 1865; Bar of L. Canada, 1866.

* Benson Estate, 1857; Cobourg Harbour Debentures, 1858; N. Halifax boundary line, 1859; McKay's will, 1861; Kingston Marine Railway, 1863; Iberville Academy, 1861; York Roads, 1865; Aylmer Parish, 1866.

† London and Port Stanley Railway (sale of land), 1858; Rouville division, 1859; Cobourg and Peterboro' Railway, 1862; Saguenay Municipality, 1863; Montreal Corporation, 1865.

‡ Mitchell incorporation, 1857; Charlevoix Registry Office, 1858; Vespra and Sunnidale separation, 1859; Waterloo registration division, 1862; King Township Treasurer, 1863; Yamaska Bridge, 1864.

§ Woodstock Woollen and Cotton Manufacturing Co., 1860; Northern Railway amendment, 1860; South Eastern Mining Co., 1861; Huguenin's admission as notary, 1861; Crevier's relief, 1863; Knowlton Cemetery, 1865; Canadian Rubber Co., 1866; Clifton Gas Works, 1867–8.

‖ Napanee incorporation, 1857; Cayuga Market block, 1863; Port Hope By-law, 1865; Church of England Synod, 1866.

¶ Montreal incorporation amendment, 1854–5; Quebec Police, 1857; Toronto Street Railway, 1861; Hamilton Debt, 1863.

Private Bill Committee,* —That the measure is one of great urgency,† or of great public utility or importance,‡ —That the notices were given for the previous Session, which was closed prematurely,§ —That Bank Charters have not heretofore been treated as private bills in New Brunswick,‖—and even, in one or two instances, on the ground that a petition had been presented against the proposed bill, which appears to have been considered as evidence that its opponents were sufficiently informed of the application.

In recommending a suspension of the Rule, however, when no sufficient notice has been given, the committee have suggested that certain matters of detail, which they considered to require notice, should not be included in the bill.¶

Up to the year 1856, it was occasionally the

---

* Durham separation, 1860; Petroleum Springs Road Co., 1861; St. Hyacinthe corporation, 1863; Lincoln County town, 1866.

† Hamilton debt consolidation, 1861; Oxford Seed Grain, 1863; Napanee Municipality, 1865.

‡ Transmundane Telegraph Co., 1859; St. Lawrence Navigation Co., 1861; North West Navigation and Railway Co., 1862.

§ Dereham Drainage, 1863; Niagara & Detroit Railway, 1865.

‖ Fredericton Bank, 1867–8.

¶ Stanstead, Shefford & Chambly Railway, 1863.

practice for the House to suspend, in a particular case, the Rule relative to Notice, upon a motion to that effect, without any previous action on the part of the Standing Orders Committee; but in that year the committee made a report, representing that the practice of indiscriminately dispensing with these notices must have a most injurious tendency, and suggesting that in future no motion for suspending the Rule in any special case be passed, until the matter in question should have been favorably reported on by the committee; this being acceded to by the House, was acted upon for the remainder of that Session. A similar recommendation made in the following year, was modified by the House so as to provide that no motion for suspending the Rule in favor of any petition be entertained, until the committee shall have reported on the subject, favorably or otherwise; and this is now provided for in the 55th Rule.

No suspension until committee has reported.

When, in any case, the notice, upon examination, proves to be insufficient, it is so reported to the House, and (unless accompanied by a recommendation to suspend the Rule) all further action in the matter is dropped; the decision of the committee being rarely overruled by the House.* One case is recorded in the Journals of the

Insufficient notice to be reported.

---

* May, p. 653.

Assembly, in which the committee, having reported the notice incomplete, recommended that it be *not* dispensed with. The House nevertheless suspended the Rule, and referred the petition back to the committee, who subsequently reported favorably, and a bill was introduced.*

Notice must be specific and clear. In judging as to the sufficiency of a notice submitted for their examination, the committee compare its terms with those of the petition, and any important variance or omission in the former is fatal either to the whole measure, or to a particular provision therein, as the case may be. In some instances the notice (though published in the prescribed manner in other respects) has been unfavorably reported on because it did not sufficiently indicate the objects sought to be attained. † This was the case with a petition for an amendment to the Act incorporating the Galt and Guelph Railway Company in 1858; on examining the petition, the amendment was found to embrace a provision for giving the holders of certain bonds issued by the company before mortgaging their road to the Great Western Railway Company, a remedy against the last mentioned company, and this not having been mentioned in the notice, it was pronounced

Galt and Guelph Railway.

---

* Huntingdon Plank Road Co., 1846.
† St. Lambert Municipality, 1861.

insufficient.*   In another instance,† upon an application for amendments to the Act dividing Chatham into two municipalities, the notice simply referred to the Act, as 19 & 20 Vic., cap. 105, without mentioning the subject, and this was pronounced insufficient.   In the same Session, the committee called the attention of the House (in one of their reports) to the utter insufficiency of a notice given in this form, and recommended " that in future, no notice be considered sufficient that does not clearly indicate the nature and subject of the¦ application."‡   This recommendation has been acted upon by the committee ever since ; and in 1862 the (51st) Rule was so amended as to require every notice to be of this character.

Chatham division.

If the notice be found too general in its terms, or if no mention be made of certain matters included in the petition which require a specific notice, the facts are specially reported, and the promoters restricted, in the details of the bill,

Petitioners restricted within the terms of the notice.

---

* In a subsequent report, five weeks later, the committee stated that the notice had since been amended, and advertised in its amended form for three weeks; and they recommended that the Rule be suspended : this was done accordingly, and a bill presented, but it was not proceeded with.

† Chatham division, 1860.   Also, Murray gravel roads, 1862; Colborne gravel roads, 1862.

‡ Assembly Journ., 1860, p. 126.

5

Exception. within the terms of the notice;* or if the matters so omitted are allowed to be inserted in the bill, due provision is made therein for the protection of all parties whose rights might be affected by the want of a specific notice.† If the notice has been given in one County or District only, the operations of the petitioners are confined to that locality.‡

Peel Manufacturing Co. In 1865, in reporting on the petition of the Peel General Manufacturing Company, for certain amendments to their charter, the committee stated that the notice was sufficient for ordinary amendments, but called the attention of the House to one of a peculiar nature, under which shareholders in the company might claim a relaxation of the Patent Laws in favor of their own inventions, when intended to be used in connection with the company. The promoters did not proceed with the bill.

In 1866, the County Council of Wellington,

---

* Port Hope Harbour, 1854-5; Vaudreuil Railway, 1854-5; St. Lawrence and Bay Chaleurs Land Co., 1857; Brockville and Ottawa Railway, 1860; Onslow Survey, 1862; Preston and Berlin Railway, 1862; Joliette incorporation, 1863; Eastern Townships Bank, 1864; De Léry Gold Mining Co., 1865; Long Point Company, 1866.

† Montreal City Loan, 1862; Buffalo & Lake Huron Railway, 1863; Tadousac Hotel Co., 1865; Bank of U. C., 1866; Clifton Suspension Bridge, 1867-8.

‡ St. Lawrence Mining Co., 1854-5.

having petitioned for an Act to legalize their By-law granting aid to a certain railway, presented a further petition, praying that the Rule requiring notice might be suspended in their case ; and the Committee on Standing Orders, having considered the last mentioned petition, reported that no sufficient reason had been urged to induce them to recommend a suspension of the Rule. Wellington By-law.

In one case* the committee reported that the notice ought not to be dispensed with, but that a bill might be introduced for the relief of the petitioner, by extending in his favor the time for appealing against a decision of the Trinity Board. The bill was accordingly introduced, but was subsequently dropped. In another case† the committee reported that a charter proposed to be amended had become void by *non user ;* and the House justified the report by taking no further action in the matter. Special Reports

In the Session of 1867-8 (after Confederation), the committee reported, with reference to two petitions, that they appeared to come more properly within the jurisdiction of the Local Legislature,‡ and they were not proceeded with.

---

* Malcolm Smith, to be reinstated as a pilot, 1859.

† North-west Transit Co., 1861 ; and again in 1862.

‡ Gore District Mutual Insurance Association, 1867-8 ; Sorghum Growers' Association of Essex, 1867-8.

(See also chapter on Legislative Jurisdiction, *supra*, p. 13.)

Other parties cannot avail themselves of a notice. It may be well to state, that the committee (though not reporting any such case to the House) has repeatedly decided that parties having a diverse interest from those by whom a notice has been published, cannot avail themselves of such notice to proceed upon their own account: among other cases, this decision was given in regard to the Sault Ste. Marie Canal in 1851, and Gage's Will case in 1862, to the knowledge of the writer.

Petitions referred back. After an unfavorable report from the committee, the House has, in a few instances,* referred petitions back to the committee, with an instruction to consider and report as to the expediency of suspending the Rule. In one case only† was their report favorable; and though in this instance the Rule was suspended, and a bill introduced, it was subsequently abandoned.

Further Report, amending a former one. It has occasionally happened, that after certain petitions have been unfavorably reported on, further evidence has been produced, sufficient to satisfy the committee. In such cases they have made a further report, amending the former one, and representing either that the notice has since

---

* Reach road allowance, 1856; Elora incorporation, 1856; Turner's contract on Brant Gaol and Court House, 1856.

† Elora incorporation, 1856.

been continued so as to complete the full time required,* or that it has been amended so as to meet the requirements of the Rule,† or that the evidence subsequently adduced proves that the notice was sufficient for all parties concerned.‡

* Hamilton & Amherstburg Railway, 1854-5 ; Peterborough School Trustees, 1857 ; St. Bonaventure Municipality, 1866.

† Galt & Guelph Railway amendment, 1858.

‡ British Farmers' Union Insurance Co. of Brantford, 1859.

7.—PRESENTATION AND FIRST READING OF BILL.

When a petition has been favorably reported
Presenta-
tion of Bill. on by the Committee on Standing Orders, a bill
may be introduced, upon a motion for leave, upon
a Monday, Wednesday or Friday, immediately
before the calling of the Orders for private
bills* (preceded, when the same is required by
the Report, by a motion to suspend the Rules).
The bill must be prepared by the promoters, in
the English and French languages, and printed
Printing. (at their expense) by the Parliamentary contractor; and 500 copies in English and 200 in French,†
must be deposited in the Private Bill Office,

---

* 56th Rule, Commons. Members of the Senate exercise
the right of bringing in bills, in that House, *without* a motion
for leave, in analogy with the practice in the House of Lords.
May, p. 439.

† The printing of the French version has been occasionally
dispensed with in bills concerning some locality within the
Eastern Townships of L. Canada.—St. Francis Bank, 1854-5;
Eastern Townships Bank, 1854-5. (In the Quebec Legislature,
the number of copies required is,—in the Legislative Council,
100 English and 250 French,—in the Legislative Assembly, 250
English and 325 French.)

and distribution thereof made before the first
reading.*   It is only in the House of Commons,
however, that bills are required to be printed at
this stage, in conformity to the Rule adopted in
1867.   In the Senate they are printed, as heretofore, before the *second* reading.†

The amount of any rates, tolls, fees or fines Rates and
inserted in the bill, must be printed in *italics* ; tolls to be
these are technically regarded by the House as in italics.
blanks, to be filled up by the committee on the
bill, and are so inserted merely to shew the
amount intended to be proposed.‡

When a bill for confirming any letters patent Bills for
or agreement is presented, a true copy of the confirming
any letters
same must be attached thereto.§   A bill of patent, or
this kind having been referred to the Private agreement.
Bill Committee in 1857, they reported that they
could not recommend that it be passed, because
no copy of the letters patent was attached.   The
omission was, however, rectified by the House, a
copy of the letters patent being attached to the
bill in committee of the whole, and it finally
received the Royal Assent.||

In 1864, several petitions relating to munici-

---

* 58th Rule, Commons.
† 58th Rule, Senate.
‡ May, p. 670.
§ 57th Rule.
|| Bessemer's Patent, 1857.

Provisions of several petitions included in one bill. palities within the same district, having been favorably reported on, the provisions of legislation sought by the different petitioners, were combined into one bill by the promoters.*

Bills informally introduced. If a bill has been informally or irregularly introduced (*i.e.*, prior to the presentation of a petition, or to the Report of the Standing Orders Committee on such petition), it may be withdrawn, with the leave of the House, and a new bill be presented in the proper course.†

Time of presentation. Private bills must be presented within the first four weeks of the Session ;‡—but this period is generally extended, to correspond with a like extension in favor of petitions. (See *supra*, p. 33.)

Reference to a standing committee, in Commons. Every private bill, when read a first time, in the House of Commons, is referred to the Standing Committee on Private Bills, the Standing Committee on Banking and Commerce, the Standing Committee on Railways, Canals, and Telegraph lines, or some other Standing Committee of a like nature : and all petitions for or against the bill§ stand referred to such com-

---

* Arthabaska and Wolfe Municipalities, 1864.

† Halifax Townships, 1859 ; Rouville Division, 1859 ; Chicoutimi Municipality, 1863; Union St. Joseph, Three Rivers, 1865.

‡ 49th Rule.

§ In the Commons of Great Britain, petitions in favor of, or against private bills, are not presented in the usual way of presen-

mittee. No bill,* originating in that House, of which notice is required to be given under the 51st Rule, can be considered, after such reference, until after ten clear days' notice of the sitting of the committee, affixed in the lobby, and appended also to the Votes. In the case of bills received from the Senate, the notice required is two days only.† Bills not requiring notice under the 51st Rule may be considered at any time after reference.

This is another of the changes effected in 1867: it was adopted with a view to expedite the proceedings on private bills, and to enable the committees to enter at an earlier period upon their labors, and so avoid the accumulation of business too often thrust upon them near the close of the Session. In the Senate, the practice in relation to the reference of bills (which, until that year, was identical in both Houses), remains as heretofore; bills are not referred until after the *second* reading,‡ and the notice to be given by the committee is one week, upon bills of the Senate,

Reference to a Standing Committee, in Senate.

---

ting petitions, but are deposited in the Private Bill Office; and all such as are deposited within a certain time after the second reading of the bill, stand referred to the committee. May, p. 685.

* 59th Rule, Commons.
† 60th Rule, Commons.
‡ 59th Rule, Senate.

and 24 hours upon those sent up from the Commons.*

Divorce Bills. Divorce Bills (which invariably originate in the Upper House) are referred (after their first reading in the Commons) to a selected committee, in place of the Standing Committee on Private Bills.† The evidence taken before the Senate (a copy of which is applied for, and communicated, by message) is referred to the committee, with power to send for persons and papers, and usually, to hear counsel.‡ The committee give two days' notice of their sitting, as in the case of other private bills.

---

* 60th Rule, Senate.

† In the British House of Commons, they are referred to " The Select Committee on Divorce Bills." May, p. 758.

‡ Harris' divorce Bill, 1841–5 ; Beresford's do., 1852–3 ; McLean's do., 1858 ; and again in 1859.

8.—PAYMENT OF FEE AND CHARGES.

Immediately after the *first reading* (or, in the Senate, after the *second reading*), and before the consideration of the bill by the committee, the fee and all other charges thereon, must be paid into the Private Bill Office. This however applies only to bills "giving any exclusive privilege, or for any object of profit, or private, corporate, or individual advantage; or for amending, extending or enlarging any former Acts in such manner as to confer additional powers." On all such bills a fee of $100 is levied, and the promoters are charged with the expense of printing 500 copies of the bill in English and 200 in French, and of printing 500 copies of the Act in English and 250 in French, with the Statutes :* this last item is subsequently refunded if the bill should fail to become law.† If the bill has not been prepared in both languages, it is charged with the cost of translation; and any additional expense incurred, for re-printing the bill in an amended form, or for printing sched-

Fee payable after first reading.

Limitation

---

* In the Province of Quebec, the numbers of copies to be provided are,—of the *Bill*,—100 English and 250 French for the Legislative Council, and 250 English and 325 French for the Legislative Assembly;—Of the *Act*,—250 English and 500 French.

† 58th Rule.

ules of tolls or other papers connected therewith, must be defrayed by the promoters. The Fee is payable only in the House in which the bill originates, and the charges for printing are made in the House in which they may be incurred. On Divorce Bills (which originate in the Upper House) the fee of $100 must be deposited in the hands of the Clerk of the Senate at the time of presenting the petition.*

Formerly the amount of the Fee charged on private bills was $60. In 1854-5, the Standing Committee of the Assembly on Contingencies reported a recommendation that the amount should be increased upon all private bills to $200; † and in 1862, the Committee on Private Bills reported‡ in favor of a scale of fees, adopting the existing rate ($60) as the *minimum*, and charging two rates on bills for raising or expending a sum amounting to $200,000 and under $400,000,—three rates when amounting to $400,000 and under $600,000, and so on in proportion ;—but no action was taken by the House on either Report.§   In

---

* 84th Rule, Senate.

† Assembly Journ., 1854-5, p. 358.

‡ 18th Report of Committee on Private Bills, L.A., 1862.

§ In the British House of Commons, every bill " for the particular benefit of any person or persons" is deemed a private bill within the meaning of the Table of Fees ; and a fee is charged at each stage of the proceedings on the petition and bill, of like

the codes of Rules adopted by the Senate and House of Commons in 1867, the amount of the fee was raised to $100.

In a few instances the fee has been refunded Refunding of fees. upon the recommendation of the Private Bill Committee, on the ground that the bill was abandoned by the promoters,*—that it amends an Act of the present Session on which the fee was already paid,†—that the fee was paid in the previous Session,‡—that the bill was rendered necessary by the legislation of the previous Session,§—that there were legal difficulties in the way of its passing,‖—that the bill has been laid aside, and a general Act substituted,¶—or that the amendments to the charter of a certain

---

amount in all cases, except that when the amount to be raised or expended is £50,000 and under £100,000, the fees payable at the 1st, 2nd, and 3rd readings (£45 in all) are doubled,—if between £100,000 and £200,000, they are tripled,—and so on in proportion. Fees are also paid by the opponents of a bill, on presenting a petition against it. Bristowe, pp. 135 to 137.

* St. Lawrence Mining Co., 1852-3; Galt & Guelph Railway, 1866; Toronto and Owen Sound Railway, 1866; Northwest Transportation Co., 1866; Canadian Mutual Life Insurance Co., 1867-8.

† Guelph lands trust, 1854-5.

‡ Johnston Estate, 1864.

§ Coyne's relief, 1865.

‖ Ayr dam and water-course (J. Watson), 1856.

¶ Various bills for admission of attorneys to practise, 1857.

6

company, were rather for the advantage of the
public than of the company.* More frequently
the fee has been refunded without the recommendation of the committee, by a motion to suspend the Rule, though the attempt has not always been successful. It has been customary,
upon the rejection or abandonment of a bill, to
refund the fees, upon a special motion being made
to that effect in the House,—but one instance of
a refusal to refund the same having occurred.†
The fees have even, in some instances, been refunded at a subsequent Session.‡

Recom-
mendation
of commit-
tee requir-
ed.

In 1863, a recommendation of the Committee
on Private Bills, that for the future, no motion for
remitting the fee upon any bill be entertained, except upon the recommendation of the
committee,§ was concurred in by the House;
and it has since been generally acted upon.

Proceed-
ings con-
tinued to
another
Session.

The Spring Session of 1863 having been brought
to a premature close, before the private business
could be completed, such of the bills (on which
the fees had been paid) as were re-introduced at
the next Session were exempted from any further
payment.‖ Arrangements were also made, in

* Provincial Insurance Co., 1858 ; U. & L. Canada Bridge
Co., 1864.

† Lake Superior Mining Co., 1852–3.

‡ Bank of Canada, 1865 (Aug. Sess.) ; Quebec Pilots, *ib.*

§ Assembly Journ., 1863 (Feb. Sess.), p. 210.

‖ Assembly Journ., 1863 (Aug. Sess.), pp. 91, 93.

the same Session (Autumn Session of 1863), by
which, in case that Session should be suddenly
closed, all private and other bills undisposed of
at the prorogation should, at the beginning of the
next Session, be at once advanced to the stage at
which they had been suspended;* and a like
arrangement was effected in the Spring Session
of 1865.†

---

* Assembly Journ., 1863, pp. 282, 288.
† Assembly Journ., 1865 (Jan. Sess.), pp. 226, 246.

9.—COMMITTEES ON PRIVATE BILLS,

AND THEIR POWERS.

Standing committees on private bills.

It has been already stated that all private bills before the House of Commons are referred, after the first reading, either to the Standing Committee on Private Bills, or to that on Banking and Commerce, or that on Railways, Canals, and Telegraph lines, or to some other Standing Committee of a similar character.* These committees are appointed early in the Session, and continue in existence until its close.† They each consist of a large

---

* In 1866, the Bill respecting the Bar of Lower Canada was referred to a *select* committee.

† This differs from the practice in the Imperial Parliament, where all railway and canal bills before the Commons are referred, after the *second* reading, to the "General Committee on Railway and Canal Bills," and all other private bills to the "Committee of Selection." The bills are classified in groups by these committees, who severally nominate special committees to consider each group, with one of their own members as chairman. (May, p. 674.) Each member of the committee on an opposed bill is required to sign a declaration that his constituents have no local interest, and that he has no personal interest in the bill, &c. *Ib.*, p. 682.)

number of members, who are nominated by a committee of selection (for all standing committees), and the nomination confirmed by the House. At their first meeting they proceed to elect a chairman. The quorum consists of a majority of the members, though of late years it has been customary for each committee, after its organization, to make a report recommending a reduction of the quorum,* which has been concurred in by the House. Members may be subsequently added by the House.

Instructions may be given to these committees by the House, concerning particular bills, or other matters.† After referring a bill, the House may if it think proper, instruct the committee to report it back before consideration.‡ The Private Bill Committee have themselves occasionally reported back bills which they thought might more advantageously be referred to another committee.§ The notice already given by the committee under the 60th Rule, has generally been declared, in such

Special Instructions.

---

* In 1859, and in each subsequent Session (up to 1867, inclusive), the quorum of the Private Bill Committee was, in this manner, reduced to *seven* members, while that of the Railway Committee was, in the Sessions between 1857 and 1861 inclusive, reduced to *nine*, but has since that time consisted of a majority of the members.

† May, p. 722.

‡ Isle Jésus Roads Co.; Terrebonne Roads Co., 1863 (Feb. Sess.); Napanee River Improvements Co., 1866.

§ Niagara District Bank, 1863.

cases, sufficient.* The Standing Committee on

Railways was, in 1852-3, instructed to consider the expediency of amending the bill for empowering the Great Western Railroad Company to construct a railroad from Hamilton to Toronto, so as to authorize them to construct a branch railway from their line to Port Dalhousie, and they reported the bill with an additional clause providing for the said branch.† The committee was again instructed in 1854-5, to enquire into the expediency of establishing a branch telegraph in the Parliament House ; which was subsequently effected, upon their report.‡ In 1863, the Standing Committee on Banking and Insurance, having under consideration a bill to repeal the Acts incorporating the Colonial Bank and certain other Banks that had forfeited their charters, made a report suggesting that they be empowered to extend their inquiries to any other banks in a like position ; and they were instructed accordingly.§ There are some general instructions given by Standing Orders of the House,

concerning all private bills, *viz.* :—to call the attention of the House to any provision that does not appear to have been contemplated in the notice, as reported on by the Committee on Standing

---

* Assembly Journ., 1863 (Feb. Sess.) p. 176 ; 1866, p. 202.

† Assembly Journ., 1852-3, pp. 290, 340.

‡ Assembly Journ., 1854-5, pp. 177, 197, 229.

§ Assembly Journ., 1863 (Aug. Sess.), p. 102.

Orders;*—to require proof in every case that the persons whose names appear in a bill for incorporating a company are of full age, and in a position to effect the objects contemplated, and have consented to become incorporated.† And in bills for confirming any letters patent, or agreement, the committee is required to see that there is a true copy of the same annexed to the bill.‡ Certain specific instructions are given by Standing Orders of the Houses of Lords and Commons, to committees on all Railway Bills,§ the object of which is, no doubt, to a certain extent attained in this country by the provisions of the General Railway clauses consolidation Act. There are also certain general instructions on all bills relating to Inclosure and Drainage, Turnpike Roads, Cemeteries and Gas Works, and Divorce cases.‖

The committee has no power to entertain questions in reference to the compliance with the Standing Orders,¶ (which pertains solely to the Standing Orders Committee) unless by special order from the House. This order is only given when the House, on the report of the Standing

No power to inquire into Standing Orders.

---

* 64th Rule.
† 62nd Rule.
‡ 57th Rule. See also May, pp. 713, 714.
§ Bristowe, p. 23.
‖ Bristowe, p. 26.
¶ Sherwood, p. 46.

Orders Committee, allow parties to proceed with
their bill on complying with certain standing
orders which they had previously neglected.*
In ordinary cases the committee merely inquire
whether the Orders of the House have been complied with; and in cases where a special report
has been made by the Standing Orders Committee

Bill must agree with the notice proved.
in reference to the extent of the notice, it is com-
pared with the powers and privileges conferred
by the bill, and if they appear to exceed the limits
of the notice, the fact is specially reported to the
House.†

Examina-tion of witnesses upon oath.
The committee has power to send for persons
and papers, and to examine witnesses upon oath,
the expenses of such witnesses being defrayed
by the parties in whose interest they have been
summoned. Prior to Confederation, the committees of either House had no power to examine
witnesses upon oath, several attempts to pass a
law to confer such a power having failed; ‡ but
in the Session of 1867–8, an Act was passed empowering the committee on any private bill, in
either House of Parliament, to examine witnesses
upon oath, to be administered by the chairman
or any member of such committee.§

---

* May, p. 707.

† 64th Rule.

‡ Assembly Journ., 1856, pp. 493, 503, 559; and 1857, pp.
31, 191.

§ 31 Vic., c. 24, sections 2 and 3.

In all questions arising before the committee, Casting vote of chairman. the chairman votes as a member, and whenever the voices are equal, he has a second or casting vote.* This provision was introduced in the revised code of Rules adopted in 1860, and is expressly limited to committees on private bills (including the Standing Committee on Private Bills, and that on Railways, and any other committee to whom private bills may be referred): it is based on Imperial practice.† The Controverted Elections Act of Canada confers the same power on the chairman of an election committee.‡

Every member present in the committee should Every member should vote. vote on all questions brought up, judging from the analogy of the practice of the House in this respect,§ and that of Election Committees under the provisions of the above mentioned Act; though in the absence of any express rule or order it may be questioned whether the committee has power to compel a member to vote who declines to do so.‖

---

* 63rd Rule.

† This practice prevails in committees of the Commons on private bills; but in the Lords' Committees the chairman votes like any other peer; and if the numbers on a division be equal, the question is negatived. May, pp. 386, 387.

‡ Consol. Stat. of Canada, Chap. 7, sec. 89.

§ May, p. 334.

‖ Frere has some excellent remarks upon this question; but

Cannot sit during sitting of the House.

The committee cannot sit during the sitting of the House; all proceedings are void after announcement that the Speaker is in the Chair.* Leave has, however, in two instances, been granted to the Committee on Private Bills to sit during the morning sittings of the Legislative Assembly,—once in 1858,† for one occasion only, and again, in 1860,‡ for the residue of the Session.§

the difference in the constitution of committees on private bills in the House of Commons, renders these remarks less applicable to the Standing Committees on private bills in this country. Frere, p. 75,—and again, on p. 84.

* Sherwood, p. 45.
† Assembly Journ., 1858, p. 658.
‡ Assembly Journ., 1860, p. 311.
§ By a Standing Order of the House of Commons of Great Britain, 21st July, 1856, it is ordered "That on Wednesdays and other morning sittings of the House, all committees shall have leave to sit, except while the House is at prayers, during the sitting, and notwithstanding the adjournment of the House." And to avoid interruption to urgent business before committees, leave is frequently obtained, on the meeting of the House in the afternoon, for a committee to sit till 5 o'clock. May, p. 388.

10.—PROCEEDINGS IN COMMITTEE ON BILL.

At each sitting, a list of the bills which are Order of considera-tion. ready for consideration is laid before the committee, in the order of their reference; and they are usually taken up in that order, unless it may be otherwise agreed upon, for the convenience of parties in attendance. In the case of opposed bills, it is customary for the parties to come to an arrangement in the Private Bill Office for the selection of a particular day for the consideration of a bill in which they are interested; and the bill, in such a case, takes precedence of all other bills appointed for that day: where no such arrangement is made, the bill is taken up in its order. It has been stated above, that no bill of Notice given by committee in certain cases. which notice by advertisement is required by the Rules, can be considered until due notice has been given by the committee.* This notice is

---

* This notice consists, in the Commons, of 10 days (affixed in the Lobby, and appended to the Votes), upon bills origina-ting in that House, and 2 days upon bills from the Upper House. (60th Rule, Commons.) In the Senate the notice

frequently reduced by the House, towards the
close of the Session, to 2 or 3 days;* but no
motion to this effect (of a general nature) can
now be entertained by the House, except upon
the recommendation of two or more of the Standing Committees charged with the consideration
of private bills.† In some instances it has been
dispensed with altogether, upon special motion, as
regards particular bills;‡ the propriety of this
course, however, has been much questioned, on
the ground of the wrong inflicted on parties who
may desire to oppose any such bill, and for whose
protection this notice is intended; and a suspension
of the Rule in this behalf is now less frequent, being
made only in urgent cases.

Parties desirous of opposing any bill before a

must be one week (affixed in the Lobby) on bills originating in
that House, and 24 hours upon bills from the Commons. (60th
Rule, Senate.)

* Assembly Journ., 1857, p. 423; 1858, p. 907; 1859, p.
271; 1860, pp. 232, 311; 1861, p. 216; 1865 (Aug. Sess.)
pp. 108, 175; 1866, p. 147.

† 60th Rule.

‡ Colonial Bank, 1858; Oshawa incorporation, 1859; Pete
boro' and Victoria land tax, 1860; London Church land, 186
(Aug. Sess.), on the recommendation of the committee, a
the request of all parties. And on the 28th May, 1862, th
Rule was suspended altogether for the residue of the Session
In 1863 (Aug. Sess.) it was suspended with reference to a
bills which had been reported on in the previous Session, whic
had closed prematurely.

committee, either on the preamble or the details, present a petition, stating the grounds of their opposition.* No such petition can be entertained that does not distinctly specify the grounds on which the petitioners object to the bill or any of its provisions. The petitioners can only be heard on the grounds so stated, and if the same are not specified with sufficient accuracy, the committee may direct a more specific statement to be given in writing, but limited to the grounds of objection which had been inaccurately specified.† No petitioners will be heard against the preamble, unless in their petition they pray to be heard against it.‡ If no parties, counsel, or agent, appear on behalf of a petition when it is

Opponents should present a petition.

And fyle appearance.

---

* In the Commons of Great Britain (as has already been stated) all petitions in favor of, or against, or otherwise relating to private bills (except the original petition for the bill, and petitions for additional provisions), are now presented by depositing them in the Private Bill Office. Every petition against a private bill, deposited not later than 10 days after the first reading, stands referred to the committee. Petitioners will not be heard before the committee unless their petition has been prepared and signed in strict conformity with the rules and orders of the House, and has been deposited within the time limited, except where they complain of any matter which may have arisen in committee, or of any proposed amendment, or additional provision. May, pp. 685, 686.

† May, p. 637.

‡ Bristowe, p. 23.

7

read, the opposition of the petitioner is held to be
abandoned.*   It is right, however, to state, with
regard to these restrictions, that although strictly
speaking they apply to all opposed bills, they are
never fully enforced by the committee, unless
the circumstances of the case appear to require it.

Counsel.   The promoters of a bill may be heard by
counsel if they desire it.†   Petitioners against
the preamble or any of the clauses may be heard
by counsel, if, in their petition, they have prayed
to be heard by themselves, their counsel, or
agent.‡   No member can act as counsel before
To what the House or before any committee; nor can any
extent
members member of either House act as counsel before the
may act. other House, on any bill depending therein,
without special permission: when such permission is given, it is understood that the gentlemen
who receive it would not be permitted to vote on

* Bristowe, p. 27.

† A Parliamentary Agent appearing before a committee of
the British House of Commons for a private bill (or upon a
petition against a bill containing a prayer to be heard by counsel) is always called on by the committee clerk to hand in the
names of two counsel, though the number of counsel who may
be heard is not limited to these.—Evidence of G. L. Smith,
Esq., Parliamentary Agent,—appended to the 3rd Report of
the Committee of the House of Commons on Private Bills,
1847. (Ans. to Ques. 913.)

‡ Standing Orders of British House of Commons relative to
Private Bills, 85.

such bill, if it should be received by the House of which they are members.* This permission has in a few instances been given to members of the Assembly,†—and once only to a member of the Legislative Council.‡

A filled up copy of the bill, containing the amendments proposed to be submitted by the promoters, must be deposited in the Private Bill Office, one clear day before the consideration of the bill.§ All parties petitioning against the bill are entitled to obtain a copy of the proposed amendments, one day before the consideration of the bill.‖

In the case of the Quebec Marine Insurance Co. in 1865 (Jan. Sess.), a petition was presented, on the part of the company, for leave to amend their bill in a matter not contemplated by the

Filled up copy of Bill to be fyled.

Amendments by promoters.

---

* May, p. 358.

† Leave was granted by the Legislative Assembly to the Hon. T. C. Aylwin, in the session of 1844-5, to appear at the Bar of the Legislative Council on the Naturalization Bill (Donegani's),—and to Messrs. Ross and Cauchon, in 1850, on the Dorchester Bridge Bill. Assembly Journ., 1844-5, p. 408; 1850, p. 261.

‡ Leave was granted by the Legislative Council, in 1843, to the Hon. Mr. Draper, to appear at the Bar of the Legislative Assembly as Counsel on the bill relating to the University of Toronto. Council Journ., 1843, p. 104.

§ 61st Rule.

‖ May, p. 682.

notice, and the Standing Orders Committee reported favorably on the petition, on the ground that the sanction of the shareholders to the amendment had been obtained. A like course was taken in regard to the Montreal Corporation bill, in the autumn Session of the same year.

Preamble read.

When the committee are about to proceed to the consideration of a private bill, the parties are called in, and the preamble is read; this being different from the practice in regard to public bills, the preamble of which is postponed until after the consideration of the clauses.* (Instances may, however, arise, in which the committee may feel it desirable that they should reserve their judgment upon the preamble until certain details of the bill have been settled: in such a case they postpone the preamble until after the consideration of the clauses; but this is of very rare occurrence.) The petitions against the bill are then read, and appearances entered

---

* This course is adopted in regard to public bills, because they are founded on reasons of state policy, and the House having affirmed the principle on the second reading, it becomes the duty of the committee not to discuss the principle again upon the preamble, but to settle the clauses first, and then to consider the preamble in reference to the clauses only. (May, p. 468.) But the expediency of a private bill being mainly founded on the allegations of fact (contained in the preamble) proof of such allegations is necessary, as a proper basis of legislation. (*Ib.* p. 718.)

upon each petition with which the parties intend to proceed.*

The promoters (or their counsel) first state their Promoters heard. case on the preamble, and then (if required) proceed to call witnesses, and to examine them. At the conclusion of this examination, when the counsel or agent for any petitioner rises to cross-examine a witness, is the proper time for taking objections to the *locus standi* of such petitioner.† It is neces- *Locus standi* of petitioners. sary that a petitioner should state the manner in which his interest is affected, in order that he may obtain a *locus standi* at all in opposition to the measure; but the grounds of objection to the bill on which he may be heard in support of such opposition, are not confined to those arising immediately out of his private interests.‡

If the committee decide in favor of his *locus standi*, he may address the committee, and produce his witnesses, and they in their turn are cross-examined by the counsel for the promoters, who has the right to reply.§ The committee may, if they please, hear petitioners against a bill on the ground

---

* May, p. 716.

† Petitioners are said to have no *locus standi* before a committee, when their property or interests are not directly and specially affected by the bill, or when, for other reasons, they are not entitled to oppose it. May, p. 690.

‡ Frere, p. 32.

§ Bristowe, p. 28.

Petitioners against a bill. of competition ;* but shareholders of a company promoting a bill are not heard in opposition unless their interest be distinct from that of the company.†

A petitioner whose interest is affected only by particular clauses in the bill, which are immaterial to the main objects of the measure, and are not referred to in the preamble, would have no right to be heard against the preamble, but only against such clauses.‡

Members required as witnesses. If the attendance of a member of the House be required as a witness, the proper course is for the chairman to write to the member requesting his attendance; if he refuse to attend, the fact is reported to the House, in order that they may take such steps in the matter as they see fit.§

Expenses of witnesses. A witness has a right to claim that his expenses be paid or guaranteed, before his examination. A witness cannot correct his evidence, except by a subsequent examination.‖

---

* May, p. 695.

† May, p. 699.

‡ Frere, p. 33.

§ Frere, p. 70. A Peer of Parliament cannot be compelled to attend a committee of the Commons, but if he attend voluntarily, it is not necessary that a message be sent to the Lords requesting his attendance, as is the case in committees on public matters. *Ib.*, p. 71.

‖ Frere, p. 72.

When counsel are addressing the committee, or while witnesses are under examination, the committee room is an open court ; but when the committee are about to deliberate, all the counsel, agents, witnesses, and strangers are ordered to withdraw, and the committee sit with closed doors. When they have decided any question, the doors are again opened, and the chairman acquaints the parties with the determination of the committee, if it concern them.*

Room cleared for discussion.'

Members of the House who are not on the committee, have a right to be present during the examination of witnesses, but not to interfere in the proceedings.† It is doubtful how far the committee has a right to exclude them from the room when cleared for discussion, but it is always customary for them to retire.

Right of members of the House to be present.

If any member insist on his right to remain, against the wish of the committee, their only course is to report the circumstances of the case to the House. ‡ If a member of the House be under examination as a witness, and the matter under consideration shall have arisen out of his

A member under examination.

---

* May, p. 715.

† By a Standing Order of the House of Lords, all Peers are entitled to attend the select committees of that House, and they are not excluded from speaking (though they be not of the committee), but they may not vote. May, p. 382.

‡ Frere, p. 74.

evidence, the right of the committee to exclude him from the room during the discussion, is less doubtful.*

Question put on preamble.

When the arguments and evidence upon the preamble have been heard, the room is cleared, and a question is put "That the preamble has been proved," which is resolved in the affirmative or the negative, as the case may be : † —If in the negative, the committee report to the House "That the preamble has not been proved to their

Preamble not proved.

satisfaction." After this decision, it is not competent for the committee to re-consider and re-verse it, but the bill should (if necessary) be re-committed for that purpose.‡

In the Imperial Parliament, the committee are

---

* The India Judicature Committee (House of Commons), in 1782, having cleared the room to deliberate on the refusal of Mr. Barwell to answer certain questions, he insisted on his privilege, as a Member of the House, of being present during the debate. The committee objected that as a party concerned in the matter under discussion, he had no right to be present. Mr. Barwell still persisting in his right, two members attended the Speaker, and returned with his opinion that Mr. Barwell had no right to insist upon being present during the debate, upon which he withdrew. The House subsequently ordered "That when any matter shall arise on which the said committee wish to debate, it shall be at their discretion to require every person not being a member of the committee to withdraw." May, p. 382.

† May, p. 720.

‡ May, p. 722.

not required to assign any reasons for thus deciding against the further progress of the bill, though the necessity for such information, to enable the House to determine upon their report, is obvious.* A different course prevails in Canada, the committee being required to state in their report† the grounds of their decision. Of these may be instanced,—That no evidence was offered in favor of the preamble, ‡ —Insufficient information or contrary evidence, § —No proof (in the petition or otherwise) of consent of the parties interested, ‖ —No proof that the majority of those whose interests would be affected are in favor of the scheme,¶—That the petitioners against the measure are as numerous as those in its favor,** or are more numerous,†† — That there is great

Reasons assigned

---

* Alpheus Todd's Report on Private Bills, 1847.

† 66th Rule.

‡ River du Chêne, 1852–3; Gatien estate, 1857.

§ Small's Pickering road allowance, 1852–3; Clarke Survey, 1857; Notre Dame du Portage Municipality, 1859; Onslow Survey, 1862.

‖ Bill to incorporate the Benevolent Societies of the Wesleyan Church, 1850; Guelph and Wellington Roads Co., 1859; Russel Estate, 1865.

¶ Hull Presbyterian Church, 1856; Quebec limits extension, 1860; Lennox and Addington separation, 1860.

** Whitby division, 1857; Stanbridge division, 1866.

†† Grey and Simcoe division, 1857; Bolton incorporation, 1858; Durham School section, 1859; Berlin town limits, 1865.

difference of opinion in the locality affected, as to
the expediency of the measure,* —That the statement of facts set forth in the preamble has been
disproved,† —That legislative interference is not
desirable or necessary,‡ —That it would interfere with law-suits pending,§ or with existing
rights,‖ —That the powers sought for would not
advance the interests of the locality,¶ —That the
✝ bill provides for an extension of the powers of a
certain company to purposes entirely foreign to
its original charter,** —That it contains most unusual provisions,†† ⚔ That a certain survey

---

* Ayr incorporation, 1857; Halifax township, 1860; Clifton division, 1866.

† Barton road allowance, 1852-3.

‡ East Hawkesbury survey, 1856; Clarke survey, 1856;
Van Norman estate, 1857; Delaware survey, 1857; York and
Peel separation, 1861 ; Quebec Stevedores incorporation, 1861 ;
Augusta Municipalities' Fund, 1862; Bruce county town, 1864 ;
Bayham by-law, 1865, and 1866 ; Montreal Licensed Victuallers,
1865.

§ Chatham survey, 1858; Peel county town, 1859; Rich-
mond Street (London) boundary line, 1861; Peterboro' and
Port Hope Railway, 1862.

‖ North-western Railway, 1856; Clifton suspension bridge,
1858; Burford survey, 1860; Hope survey, 1860; Etchemin
bridge, 1862 ; Renfrew division, 1863.

¶ St. Lawrence and Bay Chaleurs Land and Lumber Co., 1858.

** St. Clair and Rondeau Plank Road Co. amendment, 1857.

†† Metropolitan Gas and Water Co., 1857 ; Richelieu Company, 1862.

which is sought to be confirmed was not made in
conformity with the provisions of the law, * — Preamble
not proved.
That the filled-up bill submitted to the committee
differed materially from the printed bill as originally referred to them, and was not in accordance
with the petition,† —or, That it is in the power
of the Executive Government to carry into effect
the objects contemplated by the bill,‡ or the
Court of Chancery (in a bill affecting the interests
of minors).§   In one instance, in 1857, the committee reported, with reference to the bill to incorporate the St. Lawrence and Bay Chaleurs
Land and Lumber Co., that although they could
not say the preamble was not proved, yet they
could not recommend the passing of the bill, its
promoters being foreigners, residing out of the
Province.

If, upon the report of the committee concerning Committee
a certain bill, that the preamble is not proved, may be required to
the House be not satisfied with the reasons as- report evidence
signed in the report, the committee are directed to which
guided
report the reasons or evidence which guided them their decision.
in their decision ; and these, when reported, have
generally satisfied the House, so that the bill has

---

* Beverly survey, 1864.

† Toronto Esplanade, 1854-5.

‡ Bill to vest in J. Carling and others, a portion of Church
Street, London, 1852-3.

§ Watson's Ayr Mill-dam, 1856.

Bill may be referred back for amendment. proceeded no further.* If it should appear from the report, that the objection to the bill was not so much against the principle as against certain details, the committee may be instructed to amend the bill by striking out the objectionable provisions, and report the same as amended.† In one instance, however, they reported that a majority against the preamble had been obtained through one member having voted against it inadvertently; and the instruction of the House having afforded him an opportunity of correcting his vote, he had done so, and this having given a majority in favor of the preamble, the committee reported the bill.‡ In other cases, the committee having been directed to report the evidence on which their adverse decision was founded, reported the same, and it was referred to a committee of the whole, with the bill, and the bill was reported and passed.§

Alterations in preamble. It is in the power of the committee to make alterations in the preamble,‖ either by striking out or modifying such allegations as may not have

---

* Cornwall By-law, 1856; Metropolitan Gas and Water Co., 1857; St. Lawrence and Bay Chaleurs Land Co., 1858; Peterboro' and Port Hope Railway, 1862.

† Richelieu Company, 1862.

‡ Three Rivers diocese church-rate, 1852-3.

§ Clarke survey, 1857; Bruce County town, 1864.

‖ May, p. 723.

been substantiated to their satisfaction, or by ex-
punging such as the promoters may be desirous Alterations in preamble
of withdrawing;* but no new allegations or
provisions ought to be inserted, either in the preamble or the bill, excepting such as are covered
by the petition and the notice, as proved before
the Standing Orders Committee,—unless the parties have received permission from the House to
introduce such additional provisions, in compliance with a petition for leave.† Every material alteration in the preamble must be specially
reported to the House, with the reasons therefor.‡
Such alterations have almost invariably hitherto
been of a nature to limit or reduce the powers
proposed to be conferred by the bill.§ An exception was made, however, in the case of a bill
for the relief of the Ministers of a certain religious
denomination in Montreal, in 1857,‖—the preamble and provisions of which were amended so
as to apply to all ministers of that denomination
in Lower Canada; and it was passed in the

---

* Sherwood, p. 53.

† May, p. 721. See also 64th Rule.

‡ 65th Rule.

§ St. Hyacinthe incorporation, 1852-3; Upper Canada
Mining Co., 1852-3; Toronto Bank, 1854-5; Frelighsburg
Grammar School, 1857; St. Gabriel de Valcartier division, 1861;
Renfrew By-law, 1863.

‖ Bill for relief of Ministers of the Church of the "Countess
of Huntingdon's Connexion" at Montreal, 1857.

8

amended form. (But see the remarks as to the limitation of the power of the committee to make amendments, on p. 91.)

"Previous Question" cannot be put. It is a rule of Parliamentary practice, that the "previous question" cannot be put in committees, *i.e.*, that if the question were proposed that the preamble is proved, it is not competent for a member to propose the previous question "that that question be *now* put," for the purpose of voting against it. The same rule applies, of course, to the clauses, and to any amendments proposed.*

Preamble proved. When the committee have decided that the preamble has been proved, they call in the parties, acquaint them with the decision, and then go through the bill, clause by clause, and fill up the blanks; and when petitions have been presented against a clause, or proposing amendments, or for **Proceedings on clauses.** compensation, the parties are heard in support of their objections, or amendments, or claims, as they arise. Clauses may be postponed, and considered at a later period in the proceedings, if the committee think fit; or clauses which the parties have agreed to insert in the bill may, if necessary, be produced before the committee decide on the preamble.† Manuscript clauses are con-

---

* May, pp. 364, 473; Frere, p. 49.

† May, p. 720; Bristowe, p. 29.

sidered after those printed in the bill, first those proposed by the promoters, and afterwards such as may be proposed by the opponents of the bill.* If any unusual provisions are found in the bill, Unusual or any that do not appear to have been contem- provisions. plated in the notice, special mention is to be made of them in the report.†

In the case of any bill sent down from the Evidence on bills Senate, the committee, if they have not sufficient from evidence before them, can direct their chairman Senate. to move in the House that a message be sent to their Honors, requesting that the proofs and evidence on which the bill was founded may be communicated ; and these, when sent down, are referred to the committee.‡

In filling up the blanks in the bill, the commit- Rates of tee are required to insert the maximum rates toll or fees. of toll, fees, or other charges to be imposed under its provisions, which are printed in the bill in *italics*, for the information of the House, but are technically regarded as blanks.§ A practice obtained occasionally, for some years, of requiring the rates of toll proposed to be inserted in

---

* Frere, pp. 54, 61.

† Montreal Building Society ; Montreal Gas Co.; Toronto Dry Dock ; various Mining Bills : all in 1847. See also 64th Rule.

‡ Counter's stove patent, 1850; Niagara and Detroit Rivers Railroad, 1859 ; Quebec Pilots, 1860.

§ May, p. 670.

Harbour, Bridge, or Canal Bills, to be first sanctioned in a committee of the whole, and afterwards referred to the committee on the bill for insertion therein. This appears to have been the usual course prior to the Union, but upon the adoption of a system of Private Bill legislation, it was discontinued. In the Session of 1852-3, this practice was resorted to in a bill to incorporate the Port Burwell Harbour Company,* and it was subsequently observed in several instances; though it was always the exception rather than the rule. The inconvenience of this practice is most evident, as it is manifest that the committee of the whole can, at that early stage of the bill, have no sufficient evidence to guide them in establishing the rates of toll; while on the other hand, the committee on the bill have it in their power to procure all necessary information : when they report the amended bill, it is referred (after the second reading) to a committee of the whole, and an opportunity afforded to the House of exercising its judgment in the matter. Moreover tolls of this kind are imposed only upon such persons as may voluntarily use the works to be constructed under the authority of the bill, as a fair equivalent for a service rendered, and are thus altogether different in their character from a com-

---

* Assembly Journ., 1852-3, pp. 269, 285.

pulsory rate, duty, or charge upon the people, which should undoubtedly originate in a committee of the whole.* Furthermore, while the rule, as regards rates, duties, etc., inserted in public bills, is strictly observed in the Imperial Parliament, all private bills are exempt from its operation, including even those under which a local rate is proposed to be levied for a local work.† In 1862, the Committee on Private Bills presented a report, recommending that the exceptional practice referred to be discontinued,‡ and the recommendation has since been generally acted upon.

Rates of toll, &c.

The amendments made by the committee are written upon a printed copy of the bill, which is signed by the chairman, who also signs, with his

Amendments reported to the House.

---

* Three Rivers Diocese Church Rate, 1852-3.

† In 1833, a committee of the Commons (G. B.), appointed to examine into precedents in connection with this subject reported "that the general spirit of the Standing Orders and Reso-"lutions of the House, requires that every proposition to impose "a burthen or charge on any class or portion of the people, " should receive its first discussion in a committee of the whole "House. The only exception from this rule is with regard to "*tolls, rates, or duties* proposed to be levied on the subject in "*particular places* for any *local work ;* and in such cases it is " directed that no bill be ordered to be brought in till the peti- " tion for it has been referred to a committee, and they have ex- "amined the matter thereof, and reported the same to the "House." May (edition of 1844), p. 275.

‡ 18th Rep. of Com. on Private Bills, L. A., 1862.

Amendments reported to the House.

initials, each amendment made, and clause added, and another copy of the bill as amended is fyled in the Private Bill Office.* The committee, in reporting the bill, call the attention of the House to any provision that does not appear to have been contemplated in the notice,† or to any provision of an unusual character,‡ and if they have amended the bill in such a manner as to confine its provisions within the terms of the notice,§ or otherwise to restrict the same,‖ it is usually mentioned in the report. It is customary also to make special mention of any amendment of a peculiar or unusual character, as, changing the name of a proposed corporation,¶ —extending the limits of a township proposed to be erected,** —or materially altering certain arrangements provided for by the bill.†† In 1858, the

---

* 67th Rule.

† 64th Rule. See also Three Rivers Corporation, 1864.

‡ Quebec Pilots' Corporation, 1866.

§ Middlesex debt, 1854-5.

‖ Toronto and Goderich Railway, 1851; London debt, 1856; Martin's Saltfleet road allowance, 1856; Fitzroy Survey, 1863.

¶ Canadian Life and Fire Insurance Co., 1856; Colonial Bank, 1856.

** Franklin Township, 1857.

†† London town lot (Agricultural Societies), 1856; Crowland Survey, 1862; BelleIsle's relief, 1863; Foley's admission as Barrister, 1864.

committee reported a bill to detach certain lots in the township of Barton from the city of Hamilton, Special amend-ments. which they had so amended as to provide for continuing the lots in question within the limits of the city at a limited rate of taxation ; they also reported a bill to provide for the separation of the Counties of Durham and Northumberland, amended in such a manner as to leave the question of separation, &c., to the decision of the reeves and deputy reeves of the County of Durham. In 1864, they amended a bill to erect the Local Municipality of St. Colombe into a County Municipality, in such a way as merely to extend the powers of the said municipality in regard to the issuing of tavern and shop licences.

The power of the committee to make amend- Limitation of power to make amend-ments. ments is, however, limited; care must be taken in preparing them, that they involve no infrac-tion of the Standing Orders, and are not ex-cessive.* No new provisions may be intro-

---

* May, p. 681. Questions have frequently arisen (in the Imperial House of Commons) as to the right of a committee on a Railway Bill to alter the plan, which under the Standing Or-ders is required to be deposited in the Private Bill Office. The rules and practice of Parliament recognize this power, but the committee, before adopting any deviation from the line delinea-ted on the plan, require proof of the consent of the owners or occupiers through whose property the proposed deviation will pass. Sherwood, p. 57.

duced by which the interest of parties who are not suitors to the bill, or petitioners before the committee, can be affected, without due notice having been given to such parties.* If the com-

mittee consider a material alteration desirable in a particular bill (of such a nature as appears to exceed their powers), they report the bill, and suggest such alterations as may meet the supposed necessity.† In 1852–3, a bill to incorporate the Mutual Insurance Association for the Fabriques of the Diocese of Quebec, was reported, with a recommendation that the principle should be extended to each Diocese in Lower Canada; and the bill was amended accordingly, and passed. In 1860, in reporting on a bill to incorporate the Annuity and Guarantee Funds Society of the Bank of Montreal, the committee expressed their opinion that it was advisable to make it a general measure, applicable to any other Bank and its employés. The suggestion was not, however, adopted by the House, and the bill was proceeded with and passed, as a private bill. In some cases, where the committee have considered an amendment of the general law preferable to the passage of pri-

---

* Frere, p. 64.

† B. N. American Mining Co., 1847; Bill to remove the Registry Office for the County of Terrebonne, 1847. In this last mentioned case, a division of the county for registration purposes was suggested, instead of a removal.

vate acts, they have made a special report to that effect, and (occasionally) postponed the consideration of the bills to which it had reference, to afford an opportunity for the action of the House in the matter;* or, in other cases, they have expunged certain provisions, and recommended an amendment of the general law in these respects.†

In 1867-8 (after Confederation), the question of Question jurisdiction having been raised before them with of jurisdiction. regard to certain bills, they in one case ‡ solicited an instruction from the House, which, not being given, the bill was not proceeded with: in two other cases § they amended the bills and reported them, calling attention, in their report, to the doubts raised ; one of these bills was subsequently proceeded with, and the other abandoned. (See Chapter on " Legislative Jurisdiction," *ante.*) The committee have nothing to do with the title of the bill, which is only agreed to by the House after the third reading.‖

---

* Various bills for the admission of English attorneys t o practise in Canada; also various bills for incorporating Mining Companies, 1854-5. (No action was taken on the reports, and the consideration of the bills being subsequently resumed, they were reported and passed.) Joliette incorporation, 1863.

† Kingsey Falls Municipality, 1864 ; DeLéry Gold Mining Co., 1865 ; Quebec Corporation, 1865.

‡ Civil Service Building Society, 1867-8.

§ Stratford Board of Trade, and Canada Live Stock Insurance Co., 1867-8.

‖ Frere, p. 66.

Power to divide or to consolidate bills.

Power may be given to the committee by the House to divide a bill into two bills, or to consolidate two bills referred to them into one.* This last has sometimes been done by the committee, without a special Instruction.†

Abandonment of a bill by its promoters.

Every bill referred to the committee must be reported.‡ If the promoters of any bill inform the committee that they do not desire to proceed further with it, the fact is reported to the House,§ and the bill will be ordered to be withdrawn;‖ or if any other parties before the committee, either as petitioners or opponents of the bill, desire to proceed with it, the committee may permit them to do so.¶ In 1867–8, the Committee on Banking and Commerce reported, with regard to a bill to incorporate the Canadian Mutual Life Insurance Co., that the principle of mutual life

---

* Frere, p. 65.

† St. Albert de Warwick Municipality, 1863. (In 1864 several petitions relating to municipalities in Arthabaska and Wolfe, were combined into one bill by the promoters.)

‡ 65th Rule.

§ St. Lawrence Mining Co., 1852–3; Ottawa Water Works, 1866; Galt and Guelph Railway, 1866; Toronto and Owen Sound Railway, 1866; North-west Transportation Co., 1866.

‖ May, p. 726.

¶ The Manchester and Salford improvement Bill, in 1828, was abandoned in committee by its original promoters; when its opponents, having succeeded in introducing certain amendments, undertook to solicit its further progress. May, p. 633. (Note.)

insurance being new to this country, they could not recommend its adoption unless a paid up guarantee capital of at least $50,000 was provided; and as the promoters were not prepared to do this, they had abandoned the bill.

A bill, after it has been reported, may be referred back to the same committee,* or to some other committee† but this is very rarely done.

Bill may be referred back.

The evidence taken by the committee is not generally reported to the House, except in those cases where a special order to that effect may be made;‡ it is entered in a book, with the minutes of the proceedings of the committee, and kept in the Private Bill Office; but in some instances the committee have reported their proceedings without an order being made.§

Evidence not reported, without an order.

If the amendments made by the committee are so important or extensive as to render it necessary that it should be reprinted before its consideration by the House, this is done at the expense of the promoters.‖

Bill may be re-printed.

---

* Maskinongé Common, 1852-3; Strathroy and Port Frank Railway, 1857; Streetsville incorporation, 1858; Lindsay Reserve, 1859; Hamilton debt, 1863 (Aug. Sess.); St. Colombe Municipality, and other bills, 1864.

† Canadian Land and Emigration Co., 1865 (Jan. Sess.); Ashley's naturalization, *ib.*

‡ Great Southern Railway, 1857. See also *supra*, p. 83.

§ Buffalo and Lake Huron Railway, 1856; Grand Trunk Railway, 1862; Montreal and Champlain Railroad, 1864.

‖ This is required in all cases, in the Imperial Parliament, when the bill is amended. May, p. 728. (See also 56th Rule of the Legislative Council of Quebec.)

Time for
reports
limited.

The 49th Rule, while it limits the time for receiving petitions and private bills, respectively, also provides that no report of any standing or select committee upon a private bill be received after the first six weeks, but this period is invariably extended until nearly the close of the Session.

11.—SECOND READING OF BILL.

By the 66th Rule of the House of Commons, _{Time for} all private bills reported from a standing committee are placed on the Orders of the Day following the reception of the report,* for a second reading, next after bills referred to a committee of the whole House,—though they are usually taken up only on "Private Bill" days;† the only exception being in the case of bills on which the committee have reported the preamble not proven, which are not placed on the Orders of the Day at all, unless by special order of the House.

Time for second reading.

The second reading corresponds with the same stage in other bills, and in agreeing to it the House affirms the principle of the measure.‡ There is an important distinction between public

Principle of bill confirmed at this stage.

---

* In 1861, and in several subsequent Sessions, the committee, in reporting certain bills at a late period of the Session, recommended that they be placed on "the Orders of this day," which was done accordingly. Assembly Journ., 1861, p. 293, &c., &c.

† In the Legislative Assembly of Quebec, Private Bills have, by the 19th Rule, a place assigned to them on the Orders of each day.

‡ May, p. 456.

and private bills at this stage of the proceedings; a public bill being founded on reasons of public policy, the House, in agreeing to its second reading, accepts and affirms those reasons; but the expediency of a private bill is mainly founded upon allegations of fact, to be proved before a committee. It was formerly the practice, in each House, to refer the bill *after* the second reading; the affirmation of the principle of the bill, therefore, was necessary conditional, being contingent upon satisfactory proof being made of the allegations of the preamble. In 1867, the House of *Recent* Commons changed their Rule in this respect, and *change.* provided for a reference of the bill after the *first* reading,*—the second reading being postponed until after the committee had reported. By this arrangement the House is put in possession, before the second reading. of the facts of the case, and is therefore in a position to deal with the bill upon its merits. This change has not been adopted as yet, by the Senate, and bills before that House are referred, as heretofore, after the *second* reading.†

Hearing of The usual time for counsel to be heard at the *Counsel.* Bar of the House upon a bill (*pro* or *con.*) is at the second reading; but opposition has rarely been offered, hitherto, at this stage, unless upon the assumption that the principle of the proposed

---

* 59th Rule, Commons.

† 59th Rule, Senate.

measure was objectionable on grounds of public policy.* Upon four occasions only, in Canada, has counsel been heard at the Bar against the second reading of private bills.† In one instance, ‡ the House resolved (upon petitions from the parties) to hear counsel, for and against the bill, upon the question for going into committee of the whole thereon: this having been (under the arrangements then in force) the first opportunity afforded for the action of the House after the report of the committee, corresponded, in point of fact (as regarded the time for hearing opposition) with the second reading under the new arrangement. The bill having been reported by the committee with amendments, they were directed to report the evidence, and the same was printed, with the bill in its amended shape. The Order of the Day for the House in committee on the bill, being read, counsel was called in and heard: it

---

* Sherwood, p. 37. The Street Rail Com'y Bill was thrown out on the second reading, in the British House of Commons, 16th April, 1861, on notice being taken that it trenched on public rights. In England it is the duty of the Chairman of Committee of Ways and Means, under a standing order, to call the attention of the House to all such cases. Hansard's Debates, vol. 162, p. 641.

† University of Toronto (King's College) Bill, (a Ministerial private bill), 1843, 1844-5, and 1846: Montreal Consumers' Gas Co., 1846.

‡ Great Southern Railway, 1857.

was then moved " that this House will resolve itself into the said committee on this day three months :" the consideration of this motion was postponed, and the bill was subsequently abandoned. It may be here observed, that a motion to postpone the consideration of a bill for three or six months, offered at any stage, is, if agreed to, equivalent to a rejection of the bill for that Session.*

Private Bills on the Orders of the Day, in the House of Commons, are called up on Mondays, immediately after the daily routine of business; on Wednesdays and Fridays they are called for the first hour, at the evening sitting; while on Tuesdays and Thursdays they do not appear on the Orders at all.† Private Bills in the hands of members of the Administration, are placed among the "Government Orders" on Government days (Tuesdays and Fridays). In the Senate, no days are specially appointed for the consideration of private bills, but they come up from day to day, according to their relative position upon the Orders of the Day.

margin note: Private Bill days, Commons.

---

* May, p. 673.
† 19th Rule, Commons. (See note on p. 97.)

12.—PROCEEDINGS IN COMMITTEE OF THE WHOLE.

All Private Bills, after the second reading, are Reference
at once referred to a committee of the whole to committee of
House, for consideration on some future day.* whole.
Several bills may be considered in committee at
the same time.†

Counsel may be heard at the Bar of the House, Hearing of
at this or any other stage,‡ but the usual time is Counsel.
at the second reading. (See remarks on this subject, under "Second Reading of Bill," *ante*, p. 98.)

It may be well to remark here, that while it is,
of course, competent to the House to amend or

---

* This differs from the practice in the Imperial Parliament,
where such private bills as are reported without amendment are
ordered for a third reading; while those reported with amendments are referred to the Chairman of Ways and Means, and the
Speaker's Counsel, to report whether (in their amended form)
they contain the provisions required by the Standing Orders,
&c. May, p. 729.

† May, p. 467. Also, Assembly Journ., 1860, p. 445; 1861,
p. 319; 1863 (Aug. Sess.), p. 173; 1864, p. 373; 1865 (Jan.
Sess.), p. 234; 1866, p. 195.

‡ May, p. 460.

Amend-
ments of
select com-
mittees
generally
accepted
by the
House.
reject any bill after it has been reported by a select
committee, and to amend or reject any of the
amendments agreed to by the committee, practically this right is rarely exercised. The inability of the House to discuss a private bill upon its
merits in the absence of such information as evidence alone can supply, renders its reference to a
select committee indispensable; and the House
practically delegates its responsibility to that committee, and almost invariably accepts their decision. The principle thus acted upon by our
Canadian Legislature, has been established in the
Imperial Parliament as the result of a very long
experience in private bill legislation. The Right
Hon. John E. Denison, Speaker of the House of
Commons, a very high authority in all matters
connected with either public or private Parliamentary business, in his evidence before a committee of that House upon the Business of the
House, in 1861, says, in reference to this question,—" If you look at the precedent of private
Evidence
of Speaker
of H. of C.
on this
subject.
" legislation, you will see that some few years ago
" it was held that it would be quite impossible to
" concede such enormous interests as railway in-
" terests to a committee of five men; but these
" enormous interests, such as the consolidation of
" all the railways in the centre of Scotland, which
" was discussed before the House of Commons the
" other day, and the great question of the docks at

" Liverpool and the Mersey, now go to five men
" appointed by the Committee of Selection, and
" practically there is no appeal from their decision,
" because the House has been obliged almost to
" adopt as a rule that it will not interfere with the
" decision of committees."* In a subsequent
part of his evidence, after re-iterating this statement, he adds, that the House is more disposed
to support the decision of the committee, because
the smallness of the number of the members in-
creases the responsibility of the committee.†

In pursuance of this principle, the practice has
prevailed of late years, in the Lower House, in
the consideration of private bills in committee of
the whole, of not treating the amendments made
by the select committee as amendments, but considering the bill, as amended, as a whole; thus in
reporting the bill to the House, the chairman re-
fers only to the amendments made in committee of the whole. Bills from the Senate form
a necessary exception to this practice, as every
amendment made to the bill as sent down from
that House must be communicated for its concurrence.

Amendments of committee in committee of the whole.

Before the House resolves itself into committee
on a bill, an instruction may be given to the com-

---

* Report from the Select Committee of the House of Commons, on the business of the House, 1861. (Ans. to Ques. 155.)

† Same Report. (Ans. to Ques. 183 to 186 and 192.)

mittee, empowering them to make provision for
any matters not relevant to the subject matter of
the bill. An instruction is not ordinarily *compul-
sory*, but rather *permissive ;* a mandatory or com-
pulsory instruction may, however, be given, and
instances are to be found in which committees on
bills have been instructed "that they do make
provision," &c., or "do make two bills into one."*
An instruction should always be made a distinct
question, after the order of the day has been read,
and not as an amendment to the question for the
Speaker leaving the chair, unless its object be to
prevent the sitting of the committee; as the amendment, if agreed to, supersedes the question for
the Speaker leaving the Chair.† No amend-

ment which is irrelevant to the bill (as extending
its operations beyond the limits expressed in the
preamble and title, &c.) can be made without
an instruction.‡ If any amendment be made
that is not within the title of the bill, the committee amend the title accordingly, and report the
same specially to the House.§

In the Session of 1852–3, the committee of the
whole on the bill to empower the Municipal

---

* May, p. 461.

† May, p. 362.

‡ May, p. 474.

§ Standing Order, British House of Commons, 19th July,
1854. Bristowe, p. 133.

Council of the County of Two Mountains to subscribe for stock in any railway passing through that county, was instructed to inquire into the expediency of the extending its provisions to the County of Terrebonne. The bill was amended accordingly and passed, and was subsequently amended by the Legislative Council so as to extend its operation also to the counties of Rouville and Missisquoi.

When it may be found necessary to insert, in a private bill, a clause affecting the public revenue, property, or credit, the authority therefor must (with the consent of the Government) emanate from a committee of the whole: thus, in 1866, the Canada Vine Growers' Association having applied for an Act of incorporation, a bill was introduced and proceeded with in the ordinary way; and the consent of the Government having been obtained, a Resolution (originating in committee of the whole) was passed by the House, exempting the wines made by the Association from excise duties for a term of ten years; and the Resolution was referred to the committee of the whole on the bill, to make the necessary provision therein. In 1867-8, this exemption was extended for a further period of two years,—the same course being taken as before. *Clauses affecting public revenue,&c., originate in committee of whole.*

When it is intended to propose any important amendment in committee of the whole, or at the *Notice to be given of amendments.*

third reading, one day's notice thereof must be given.*

Course of proceeding in committee of the whole. In the committee of the whole, the same course is adopted as in the select committee,—the question being proposed on the preamble first.† The chairman then reads the number of each clause in succession, with the marginal note which explains its objects. If no amendment be offered to a clause, he at once puts the question, "That this clause stand part of the bill," and proceeds to the

Amendments. next. When an amendment is proposed, he states the line in which the alteration is to be made, and puts the question in the ordinary form. No amendment can be made to a clause after the committee has passed on to another clause; nor can any amendment be offered to any clause which is irrelevant to the subject matter of such clause, but the same should be submitted, as a separate

Clauses postponed. clause, at the end of the bill.‡ Clauses may be postponed, unless they have been amended, when it is not regular to postpone them. Postponed

---

* 68th Rule. In the Commons of G. B., every such amendment is also, in all cases involving a necessity therefor, referred to the Committee on Standing Orders for their report. May, p. 728.

† In this respect differing from the course pursued upon public bills, the preamble of which is postponed until the clauses have been settled.

‡ May, p. 469.

clauses are considered after the other clauses are
disposed of, and before any new clauses are
brought up. If the committee cannot go through **Report.**
the whole bill at one sitting, they direct the chairman to report progress, and ask leave to sit again.
When the bill has been fully considered, the
chairman puts a question, "That I do report this
bill without amendment," or "with the amendments, to the House;" which being agreed to, the
sitting of the committee is concluded, and Mr.
Speaker resumes the chair: upon which the
chairman approaches the steps of the Speaker's
chair, and reports from the committee that "they
had gone through the bill and had made amendments thereto," or that "they had gone through
the bill and directed him to report the same
without amendment." * Sometimes, however,
the proceedings of a committee are brought to a
close by an order "That the chairman do now
leave the chair;" in which case the chairman,
being without instructions, makes no report to the
House, and the bill disappears from the Order
Book and is generally regarded as defunct; but
it is nevertheless competent for the House to appoint another day for the committee, and to proceed with the bill.†

---

* May, p. 476.
† May, p. 476.

When the chairman has reported the bill to the House, the entire bill is open to consideration, and amendments may be made, and new clauses added (of which due notice has been given, as above mentioned), or the bill may be re-committed for further amendment.* If amendments have been made in committee, the question is at once put upon each amendment, in the order in which it stands in the bill; or the consideration of the bill, as reported, may be postponed to a future day. If any of the amendments are supposed to be in excess of the Notice given by the promoters of the bill, the proper course is to refer them to the Committee on Standing Orders for their report.†

Proceedings after report.

When the bill has been reported, and the amendments made in committee (if any) have been disposed of by the House, it is ordered for a third reading on the following day. The practice of engrossing on parchment, all bills ordered for a third reading, was discontinued in 1851, when both Houses agreed to substitute bills printed by the Queen's Printer, for the engrossed copies : a further change was made in 1862, when the printing of these bills was transferred to the Parliamentary contractors, with whom it still remains.

Third reading ordered.

---

* May, p. 478.

† Ottawa & Prescott Railway, 1865 (Jan. Sess.); Cobourg & Peterboro' Railway, 1865 (Aug. Sess.)

13.—THIRD READING OF BILL.

Private bills on the Orders of the Day for a third reading, take precedence, on Private Bill days (see remarks under "Second reading of Bill" *supra*, p. 100) of all other Orders.* At this stage it is not customary to make any amendments but such as are merely verbal; no important amendment may be proposed without one day's notice thereof:† if it be considered necessary, the order for the third reading may be discharged, and the bill re-committed. {Time for third reading.}

This is usually the stage at which the Queen's consent is signified to any bill affecting the property or interests of the Crown.‡ {Rights of the Crown.}

The order for the third reading being read, the member in charge of the bill moves, 1st, " That the bill be now read a third time; 2nd, " That the bill do now pass, and that the title be," &c. The {Passage of bill.}

---

* 20th Rule, Commons.   48th Rule, Senate.
† 68th Rule (both).
‡ May, p. 732.

10

Clerk is then ordered to carry the bill to the Senate, and desire their concurrence.

Every stage of a private bill, in its passage through the House of Commons, has now been described. It may be here mentioned, that, in accordance with the practice on public bills, a bill may, upon urgent and extraordinary occasions, be advanced two or more stages in one day,* but except in cases of urgent and pressing necessity, no motion may be made to dispense with any Standing Order relative to private bills without due notice,† printed in the Votes.

No Standing Order suspended without notice.

Bills amended by Senate. If a bill be subsequently returned from the Senate with amendments, the member in charge (or any other member acting for him) moves " That the amendments made by the Senate to the Bill (*title*) be now taken into consideration." They are then read by the Clerk a first time, and if merely verbal or unimportant, they are read a second time, and may be at once agreed to; the Clerk is then ordered to carry the bill to the Senate. If any of the amendments be important, they are referred to the Standing Committee to which the bill was originally referred,‡ and all further pro-

Amendments referred, in certain cases.

---

* 43rd Rule.

† 70th Rule.

‡ 69th Rule. See Guelph & Lake Huron Railway, 1864; St. Charles Bridge, 1866: Port Hope, Lindsay & Beaverton Railway, 1866.

ceedings on the matter are suspended until their
report is received.

The practice in the Senate with reference to **Bills amended by Commons.**
any of their bills which may have been returned
from the Commons with amendments, differs
somewhat from that of the Commons in this respect,—leaving it optional to refer the amendments to the select committee, or to a committee
of the whole.*

If the House disagree to one or more of the **Amendments disagreed to.**
amendments, a committee is appointed to draw
up the reasons for disagreeing, and they are communicated to the Senate at a conference,† and
an opportunity is thus afforded to the Senate of
not insisting upon the amendments objected to;
or the reasons may be set forth in the motion for
disagreeing, and communicated by message.‡ In
the event of both Houses refusing to yield the
point in discussion, the bill is withdrawn or abandoned.§

In case a bill should not be proceeded with in **Bills not proceeded with in Senate.**
the Senate, in consequence of amendments having
been made which infringe the privileges of the
Lower House, the same proceedings are adopted

---

* 69th Rule, Senate.

† Levis incorporation, 1861.

‡ Quebec Corporation, 1866.

§ Sherwood, p. 74.

as in case of a public bill. A committee is appointed to search the Journals of the Senate, and
on their report, another bill may be ordered, including the amendments made by the Senate.*

Committee to search Journals.

---

* May, p. 733.

14.—PROCEEDINGS ON PRIVATE BILLS IN THE SENATE.

The proceedings on private bills in the Upper House differed materially from those in the Lower House, until the year 1861; but in that year the Legislative Council adopted Private Bill Rules identical with those of the Legislative Assembly. Some changes were made in these Rules by the House of Commons, in the first Session after Confederation,—the most important of which consisted in the reference of bills after the *first* instead of the *second* reading (hereinbefore referred to): this change, and certain minor alterations contingent upon it, were not adopted by the Senate, and bills before that House are therefore referred, as heretofore, after the second reading. In other respects the proceedings of the two Houses may be said to be identical.* When any such bill has been

Proceedings nearly identical with those of Commons.

Exception.

---

* The House of Lords have certain Standing Orders which are not common to both Houses. By one called the "Wharncliffe Order," it is provided that no bill empowering an existing company to execute or contribute to works, other than those for which it was originally constituted, or for the amalgamation,

Evidence. referred to a select or standing committee, the same course is taken for obtaining evidence upon the preamble; or the committee can, if they desire it, instruct their chairman to move that a message be sent to the Commons, requesting that the proofs and evidence on which the bill is founded may be communicated,* and these, when received, are referred to the committee.

Notice of sitting of committee. In the case of bills upon which notice by advertisement is required by the Rules, the committee give twenty-four hours' notice of their sitting.†

Origination of bills in either House. By far the greater number of private bills are introduced first in the Commons, but no arrangement has yet been effected between the two Houses, similar to that in operation in the Imperial Parliament, for regulating the class of bills wheih should originate in each House. A reference to

---

dissolution, or abandonment of the company, will be allowed to proceed without proof that a meeting of the proprietors was held, at which the bill was approved. There are also (under other of their Standing Orders) special matters required to be proved, or to be done, in certain classes of bills; and it is especially provided that no bill for the regulation of any trade, or the extension of the term of a patent, is to be read a second time, until a select committee has reported upon the expediency of taking it into further consideration. May, pp. 733 to 740.

* Pickering Harbour and Road Bill, 1852-3; Bill to remedy defects in title to Lot 1, Broken concession A and B, township of Hamilton, 1854-5.

† 60th Rule, Senate.

the remarks on this subject in the Preliminary
Chapter, and the corresponding Note, will ex-
plain the nature of this arrangement. (*supra*, p. 5.)

Divorce Bills* are introduced first in the Senate, DIVORCE BILLS:
and there are certain Standing Orders concerning
them which are peculiar to that House. On the
presentation of the petition, a sum of $100 is de- Fee.
posited in the hands of the Clerk,† in place of
the fee levied upon other private bills after the
second reading. Notice of the application must
be published in the Official Gazette, and in two Notice.
other newspapers, during six months before the
presentation, instead of two months,‡ and various
matters must be proved on the reading of the
petition, which are specified in detail in the Chapter headed " Proof of Notices," &c. (*supra*, p. 38.)
The bill, when presented, cannot be read a First and second
second time until 14 days shall have elapsed from reading of
the first reading : a notice of the day appointed bill.
therefor, with a copy of the bill, are served on the
party from whom the divorce is sought ; and
proof, on oath, of such service (where the same is
possible) is adduced at the Bar before the second
reading.§ The petitioner attends below the Attendance of
Bar, at the second reading, to be examined gene- petitioner.
rally, or as to any collusion between the parties

---

* The remarks concerning Divorce Bills, and bills for the reversal of Attainders, are inapplicable to the Legislature of Quebec.
† 84th Rule, Senate.
‡ 73rd Rule, Senate.
§ 77th Rule, Senate.

to obtain a separation, unless such attendance is dispensed with.* After the second reading, **Examination of witnesses.** witnesses are examined at the Bar, on oath, in support of the bill, the preliminary evidence being that (by certificate or otherwise) of the due celebration of the marriage of the parties.† The **Counsel.** counsel for each party may be heard at the Bar, either on the evidence, or on the provision for the future support of the wife.‡ Witnesses are **Summons for witnesses.** notified by a summons under the hand and seal of the Speaker, served at the expense of the party applying therefor, by whom also their expenses are defrayed.§ Any witness refusing to attend is taken into the custody of the Usher of the Black Rod, and is liable for all expenses attending such **Bill referred to committee of whole.** default.‖ After the second reading, the bill is referred, not to a select or standing committee, but to a committee of the whole House.¶ No **Prohibitory clause.** bill to dissolve a marriage on the ground of adultery is received, without a clause prohibiting the offending party from marrying; but this clause is struck out in committee, or on the report, except in very peculiar cases.** In all subsequent

---

* 78th Rule, Senate.
† 79th Rule, Senate.
‡ 80th Rule, Senate.
§ 81st Rule, Senate.
‖ 82nd Rule, Senate.
¶ May, p. 757.
** May (Edit. of 1855), p. 611.

proceedings, divorce bills are dealt with in the same manner as other private bills. If any mat- Unprovided cases. ter not provided for by the Rules should arise, reference is had to the Rules and practice of the House of Lords.* When the bill is reported, and any amendments that may have been made are disposed of by the House, it is ordered to be read a third time on a future day, when it is read a third time, passed, and sent to the Commons in the usual form.

Bills for the reversal of attainders, or for the re- Reversal of attainders, &c. storation of honors and lands, are first signed by the Governor General, and are presented in the Senate (without a previous petition) by command of His Excellency;† after which they pass through the ordinary stages, and are sent to the Commons. Here the Queen's consent is signified before the first reading; and if this form be overlooked, the proceedings will be null and void. After the second reading,‡ they may be ordered to be read a third time on a subsequent day, without reference to a committee. Such bills receive

---

* 85th Rule, Senate.

† Matthews' attainder reversal; Council Journ., 1846, p. 147.

‡ In the British House of Commons, such bills, after the second reading, are committed to several members specially nominated, "and all the members of this House who are of Her Majesty's most honorable Privy Council, and all the gentlemen of the long robe." May, p. 750.

the Royal Assent in the usual form, as public bills.*

The bills sent down to the Commons pass
Proceed-
ings in
Commons
on bills
from
Senate. through the same stages, and are subject to the same rules, as other private bills, except that divorce bills are referred to a selected instead of a standing committee. When any private bill (not being a divorce bill)† is so received, that is not based on a petition which has been already reported on by the Committee on Standing Orders, it is taken into consideration and reported on by the said committee, after the first reading,‡ with reference to the notices required by the Rules.

---

* May, p. 751.
† May, p. 757.
‡ 54th Rule.

15.—ROYAL ASSENT.

Private bills receive the Royal Assent in the *"Public Act" clause.* same manner and form, and at the same time, as public bills. Heretofore, every private Act, almost without exception, contained a clause declaring that it "shall be deemed a public Act." The effect of this clause was that it should be construed as an enactment that such Act should be judicially noticed by all Judges, Justices of the Peace and others, without being specially pleaded; whereas private Acts which did not contain such a clause could be judicially noticed only when specially pleaded. But by the "Interpretation Act" passed in 1867, it is expressly provided that "every Act shall, unless by express provision it is declared to be a Private Act, be deemed to be a Public Act, and shall be judicially noticed by all Judges, Justices of the Peace, and others, without being specially pleaded ; and all copies of Acts printed by the Queen's Printer, shall be evidence of such Acts and of their contents." *

All Acts now deemed to be Public Acts.

---

* 31 Vic., cap. 1, sec. 7., sub.-sec. (A similar provision was made by the Legislature of Quebec, in the " Interpretation Act," 31 Vic., cap. 7, sec. 6.)

Printing of private acts with the Statutes.

Until the year 1849, private Acts were printed with the public statutes, and bound together in the same volume. In that year, an Act was passed* which provided that local Acts should be printed (at the expense of the Province) in such number only as should suffice for distribution to the Judges, Public Departments, and certain local functionaries; and that of private or personal Acts, 150 copies only should be printed, at the expense of the parties obtaining the same. Under this arrangement no private Acts of any class were printed for general distribution with the Statutes; and the inconvenience attending it was so strongly felt, that in 1851 an Act was passed† providing for the printing and distribution of all local, private, and personal Acts, in the same manner, and to the same extent as the public Acts,—reviving, in fact, the former practice of binding up all the Acts of a Session, public and private, in the same volume. But by the "Interpretation Act" of 1867, it is provided that the Governor in Council may direct the distribution of the Statutes in such manner, either by the binding of the Public General Acts, and Acts of a local or private character, in separate volumes, or by binding them together in the same volumes

---

* 12 Vic., cap. 16.

† 14, 15 Vic., cap. 81.

with separate indexes or otherwise, as may be deemed expedient.* It may be worthy of consideration whether the public convenience would not be sufficiently consulted by printing a limited number (say 500 copies) of the local and private Acts, binding them in a supplementary volume, and distributing them with the public Acts only where they are really required.† This would cause a large saving in the cost of printing, and would disencumber the Statute Book of a mass of enactments which have no bearing on the statute law of the land.

---

* 31 Vic., cap. 1, sec. 13.

† All such private Acts of the Imperial Parliament as contain the "public" clause are printed in a separate collection, and are known as local or personal Acts. Another class, consisting chiefly of inclosure, drainage, and estate Acts, are printed by the Queen's Printers, and contain a clause declaring that a copy so printed "shall be admitted as evidence thereof by all judges, justices and others," and a further enactment that the "Act shall not be deemed a public Act." A third class, consisting of name, naturalization, divorce, and other strictly personal Acts, are not printed; but a list of them is inserted by the Queen's Printers after the titles of the other private Acts. May, pp. 759, 760.

11

APPENDIX I.

RULES COMMON TO BOTH HOUSES

IN RELATION TO

PRIVATE BILLS.

NOTE.—The Rules of the Legislative Council and Legislative Assembly of Quebec correspond with these, except that the Rules of the Council are numbered from 47 to 70; some little variation occurs in respect to the printing of bills, which is referred to in its place.

Petitions for Private Bills. 49. No Petition for any Private Bill is received by The House [Senate] after the first three weeks of each Session; nor may any Private Bill be presented to The House [Senate] after the first four weeks of each Session; nor may any Report of any Standing or Select Committee upon a Private Bill be received after the first six weeks of each Session. [And no Motion for the general suspension or modification of this Rule shall be entertained by The House, unless after reference made thereof at a previous sitting of The House, to the several Standing Committees charged with consideration of Private Bills, or upon Report submitted by two or more of such Committees.]*

---

* This sentence occurs in the Commons Rule only.

50. The Clerk of The House [Senate] shall, during each Recess of Parliament, publish weekly in the Official Gazette, the following Rules respecting Notices of intended applications for Private Bills, and in other newspapers (English and French) the substance thereof; and shall also, immediately after the issue of the Proclamation convening Parliament for the despatch of business, publish in the Official Gazette, and in other newspapers, as aforesaid, until the opening of Parliament, the day on which the time limited for receiving Petitions for Private Bills will expire, pursuant to the foregoing Rule; and the Clerk shall also announce, by notice affixed in the committee rooms and lobbies of this House [the Senate] by the first day of every Session, the time limited for receiving Petitions for Private Bills, and Private Bills, and Reports thereon.

Publication by the Clerk, of Rules relative to Notice, &c.

51. All applications for Private Bills, properly the subjects of legislation by the Parliament of Canada within the purview of "The British North America Act, 1867," whether for the erection of a Bridge, the making of a Railroad, Turnpike Road, or Telegraph Line; the construction or improvement of a Harbour, Canal, Lock, Dam or Slide, or other like work; the granting of a right of Ferry; the incorporation of any particular Trade or Calling, or of any Banking or other Joint Stock Company;* or otherwise for granting to any

Notices for Private Bills.

---

* The Quebec Rule omits "Banking," and substitutes various local matters under Provincial jurisdiction.

individual or individuals any exclusive or peculiar rights or privileges whatever, or for doing any matter or thing which in its operation would affect the rights or property of other parties, or relate to any particular class of the community; or for making any amendment of a like nature to any former Act,—shall require a Notice, clearly and distinctly specifying the nature and object of the application, to be published as follows, viz.:—

Notices for Private Bills. *In the Province of Quebec*—A Notice inserted in the Official Gazette, in the English and French languages, and in one newspaper in the English, and one newspaper in the French language, in the District affected, or in both languages if there be but one paper; or if there be no paper published therein, then (in both languages) in the Official Gazette, and in a paper published in an adjoining District.

In any other Province—A Notice inserted in the Official Gazette, and in one newspaper published in the County, or Union of Counties, affected, or if there be no paper published therein, then in a newspaper in the next nearest County in which a newspaper is published.

Such Notices shall be continued in each case for a period of at least two months, during the interval of time between the close of the next preceding Session and the consideration of the Petition.

52. Before any Petition praying for leave to bring in a Private Bill for the erection of a Toll-bridge, is presented to the House [Senate], the person or persons intending to petition for such Bill, shall, upon giving the Notice prescribed by the preceding Rule, also, at the same time, and in the same manner, give Notice of the Rates which they intend to ask, the extent of the privilege, the height of the arches, the interval between the abutments or piers for the passage of rafts and vessels, and mentioning also whether they intend to erect a drawbridge or not, and the dimensions of the same.

Toll Bridge Bills.

53. Petitions for Private Bills, when received by The House [Senate], are to be taken into consideration (without special reference) by the Committee on Standing Orders; which is to report in each case, whether the Rules with regard to Notice have been complied with; and in every case where the Notice shall prove to have been insufficient, either as regards the Petition as a whole, or any matter therein which ought to have been specially referred to in the Notice, the Committee is to recommend to The House [Senate] the course to be taken in consequence of such insufficiency of Notice.

Petitions to be reported on by Standing Orders Committee

54. All Private Bills from the Senate [House of Commons], (not being based on a Petition which has already been so reported on by the Committee)

Private Bills from Senate.

shall be first taken into consideration and reported on by the said Committee in like manner, after the First Reading of such Bills, and before their consideration by any other Standing Committee.

Suspension of Rules.

55. No Motion for the suspension of the Rules upon any Petition for a Private Bill is entertained, unless the same has been reported upon by the Committee on Standing Orders.

Introduction of Private Bills.

56. All Private Bills are introduced on Petition, and presented to The House [Senate], [upon a motion for leave, to be made on a Monday, Wednesday, or Friday, immediately before the calling of the Orders for Private Bills,—and *] after such Petition has been favorably reported on by the Committee on Standing Orders.

Letters Patent, or Agreements.

57. When any Bill for confirming any Letters Patent or Agreement is presented to The House, [Senate] a true copy of such Letters Patent or Agreement must be attached to it:

Fees, and cost of preparing and printing Private Bills.

58. The expenses and costs attending on Private Bills giving any exclusive privilege, or for any object of profit, or private or corporate or individual advantage; or for amending, extending, or enlarging any former Acts, in such manner as to confer additional powers, ought not to fall on the public; accordingly the parties seeking to

---

* These words occur in the Commons Rule only. (In the Rule of the Legislative Assembly, the limitation to Monday, Wednesday and Friday, is omitted.)

obtain any such Bill, shall be required to pay into Fees and charges. the Private Bill Office the sum of one hundred dollars, immediately after the [First Reading *] thereof: and all such bills shall be prepared in the English and French languages, by the parties applying for the same, and printed by the Contractor for printing the Bills of The House [Senate], and 500 copies thereof in English and 200 copies in French† shall be deposited in the Private Bill Office [and distribution thereof made, before the First Reading ‡]; and no such Bill shall be read a Third time until a certificate from the Queen's Printer shall have been fyled with The Clerk, that the cost of printing 500 copies of the Act in English and 250 in French,§ for the Government, has been paid to him.

The Fee payable on the [First Reading *] of Fee, and cost of printing, where paid. any Private Bill is paid only in the House in which such Bill originates, but the cost of printing the same is paid in each House.

59. Every Private Bill, when read a [First time Bills and Petitions referred. ‖] is referred to the Committee on Private Bills, if any such shall have been appointed, or to some other Standing Committee of the same character;

---

* "*Second* reading," in Senate Rule.

† In the Quebec Rule these numbers are 100 English and 250 French (Legislative Council),—and, 250 English and 325 French (Legislative Assembly).

‡ In the Senate Rule, the words "before second reading," occur in place of those between brackets.

§ In the Quebec Rule,—250 English and 500 French.

‖ "*Second* time," in Senate Rule.

and all Petitions before The House [Senate] for or against the Bill are considered as referred to such Committee.

COMMONS.	SENATE.

Sitting of Committee

60. No Committee on any Private Bill, originating in this House, of which Notice is required to be given, is to consider the same until after ten clear days' Notice of the Sitting of such Committee has been first affixed in the Lobby; nor, in the case of any such Bill originating in the Senate, until after two days' like Notice. And no Motion for any general suspension or modification of this Rule, shall be entertained by the House, unless after reference made thereof at a previous sitting of The House, to the several Standing Committees charged with consideration of Private Bills, or upon Report submitted by two or more of such Committees.

2. On the day of the posting of any Bill under this Rule, the Chief Clerk of the Private Bill Office, shall append to the printed Votes and Proceedings of the day, a Notice of such posting : and he shall also append to the Votes of each day, a Notice of the meetings of any of the Standing Committees charged with the consideration of Private Bills or Petitions therefor, that may have been appointed for the following day.

61. A copy of the Bill containing the Amend-

SENATE.

60. No Committee on any Private Bill originating in the Senate, of which Notice is required to be given, is to consider the same until after a week's notice of the Sitting of such Committee, has been first affixed in the Lobby ; nor, in the case of any such Bill originating in the House of Commons, until after twenty-four hours' like notice.

ments proposed to be submitted to the Standing Committee, shall be deposited in the Private Bill Office, one clear day before the meeting of the Committee thereupon.

62. All persons whose interest or property may be affected by any Private Bill, shall, when required so to do, appear before the Standing Committee touching their consent, or may send such consent in writing, proof of which may be demanded by such Committee. And in every case, the Committee upon any Bill for incorporating a Company, may* require proof that the persons whose names appear in the Bill as composing the Company, are of full age, and in a position to effect the objects contemplated, and have consented to become incorporated.

63. All questions before Committees on Private Bills are decided by a majority of voices, including the voice of the Chairman; and whenever the voices are equal, the Chairman has a second or casting vote.

64. It is the duty of the Select Committee to which any Private Bill may be referred by The House [Senate], to call the attention of The House [Senate] specially to any provision inserted in such Bill that does not appear to have been contemplated in the Notice for the same, as reported upon by the Committee on Standing Orders.

---

* In the Rule of the Legislative Council of Quebec, " shall " is substituted for " may."

Report of Committee   65. The Committee to which a Private Bill may have been referred, shall report the same to The House [Senate], in every case ; and when any material alteration has been made in the Preamble of the Bill, such alteration, and the reasons for the same, are to be stated in the Report.

Preamble not proved.   66. When the Committee on any Private Bill report to The House [Senate] that the Preamble of such Bill has not been proved to their satisfaction, they must also state the grounds upon which they have arrived at such a decision ; and no Bill so reported upon shall be placed upon the Orders of the Day unless by special order of The House [Senate].

[2. Private Bills otherwise reported to The House by such Committee, shall be placed upon the Orders of the Day following the reception of the Report, for a second reading, in the proper order, next after Bills referred to a Committee of the Whole House.*]

Chairman to sign Bills and Amendments.   67. The Chairman of the Committee shall sign with his name at length, a printed copy of the Bill, on which the Amendments are fairly written, and shall also sign with the initials of his name, the several Amendments made and Clauses added in Committee ; and another copy of the Bill, with the amendments written thereon, shall be prepared by the Clerk of the Committee, and fyled

---

* This paragraph occurs in the Commons Rule only.

in the Private Bill Office, or attached to the Report.

68. No important Amendment may be proposed to any Private Bill, in a Committee of the Whole House, or at the Third Reading of the Bill, unless one day's notice of the same shall have been given. *Amendments by the House.*

69. When any Private Bill is returned from the Senate [House of Commons] with amendments, the same not being merely verbal or unimportant, such amendments are, previous to the Second Reading, referred to [a Committee of the Whole, or to *] the Standing Committee to which such Bill was originally referred. *Bill amended by Senate.*

70. Except in cases of urgent and pressing necessity, no Motion may be made to dispense with any Standing Order relative to Private Bills, without due notice thereof. *Dispensing withStanding Orders.*

71. A Book, to be called the "Private Bill Register," shall be kept in a room to be called the "Private Bill Office," in which Book shall be entered, by the Clerk appointed for the business of that Office, the name, description, and place of residence of the parties applying for the Bill, or of their agent, and all the proceedings thereon, from the Petition to the passing of the Bill; such entry to specify briefly each proceeding in The House [Senate], or in any Committee to which *Private Bill Register.*

---

* These words occur in the Senate Rule only.

the Bill or Petition may be referred, and the day on which the Committee is appointed to sit. Such book to be open to public inspection daily, during Office hours.

'Private Bill Committees.

72. The [Chief*] Clerk of the Private Bill Office shall prepare, daily, lists of all Private Bills, and Petitions for such Bills, upon which any Committee is appointed to sit, specifying the time of meeting and the room where the Committee shall sit; and the same shall be hung up in the Lobby.

(The following Rules may also be given, as bearing on the practice in Parliament in relation to Private as well as Public Bills.)

(Senate.)

Unprovided cases, Senate.

113.—In all unprovided cases, the rules, usages, and forms of the House of Lords are to be followed.

(Commons.)

Parliamentary Agents.

73.—Every Parliamentary Agent conducting proceedings before the House of Commons, shall be personally responsible to the House and to the Speaker for the observance of the rules, orders and practice of Parliament, and rules prescribed by the Speaker, and also for the payment of all fees and charges; and he shall not act as a

---

* In Commons Rule only.

Parliamentary Agent until he shall have received the express sanction and authority of the Speaker.

74.—Any Agent who shall wilfully act in violation of the rules and practice of Parliament, or of any rules to be prescribed by the Speaker, or who shall wilfully misconduct himself in prosecuting any proceedings before Parliament, shall be liable to an absolute or temporary prohibition to practise as a Parliamentary Agent, at the pleasure of the Speaker; provided that upon the application of such Agent, the Speaker shall state in writing the ground for such prohibition. *Agents violating Rules liable to suspension.*

116.—In all unprovided cases, the rules, usages and forms of the House of Commons of the United Kingdom of Great Britain and Ireland shall be followed. *Unprovided cases, Commons.*

APPENDIX II.

RULES OF THE SENATE

CONCERNING

BILLS OF DIVORCE.

Divorce notices published.

73. Every Applicant for a Bill of Divorce is required to give Notice of his intended application, and to specify from whom and for what cause, by advertisement during six months, in the *Official Gazette*, and in two newspapers published in the District, in Quebec, or County or Union of Counties in the other provinces, where such Applicant usually resided at the time of the separation, or if the requisite number of papers cannot be found therein, then in the adjoining District, or County or union of Counties.

The Notice for the Province of Quebec, is to be published in the English and French languages.

And served on ad-

74. A copy of the Notice, in writing, is to be served, at the instance of the Applicant, upon

the person from whom the Divorce is sought, if verse party. the residence of such person can be ascertained; and proof on Oath of such service, or of the attempts made to effect it to the satisfaction of The Senate, is to be adduced before The Senate on the reading of the Petition.

75. When Proceedings in any Courts of Law have taken place prior to the Petition, an exemplification of such Proceedings to final judgment, duly certified, is to be presented to The Senate, on the reading of the Petition.

Proceedings in Courts filed.

76. In cases where damages have been awarded to the Applicant, proof on Oath must be adduced, to the satisfaction of The Senate, that such damages have been levied and retained, or explanation given to The Senate for the neglect or inability to levy the same under a writ of execution, as they may deem a sufficient excuse for such omission.

Damages levied.

77. The Second Reading of the Bill is not to take place until fourteen days after the first reading, and Notice of such second reading is to be affixed upon the Doors of The Senate during that period, and a copy thereof, and of the Bill, duly served upon the party from whom the Divorce is sought; and proof, on Oath, of such Service, adduced at the Bar of The Senate, before proceeding to the second reading, or sufficient

Formalities before 2nd reading.

proof adduced of the impossibility of complying with this regulation.

78. The petitioner is to appear below the Bar

of The Senate, at the second reading, to be examined by the Senate, generally, or as to any collusion or connivance between the parties to obtain such separation, unless The Senate think fit to dispense therewith.

79. After the Second Reading, Witnesses are to

be heard at the Bar of The Senate on Oath; the preliminary evidence being that of the due celebration of the marriage between the parties, by legitimate testimony, either by witnesses present at the time of the marriage, or by complete and satisfactory proof of the certificate of the officiating minister or authority.

80. The Counsel for the Applicant, as well as

the party from whom the Divorce is sought, may be heard before the Bar of The Senate, as well on the evidence adduced, as on the provisions for the future support of the wife, if deemed necessary.

81. The Witnesses are notified to attend by a

Summons, to issue under the hand and seal of The Speaker, to the parties applying for the same, on application to The Clerk of The Senate, and served at the expense of the said parties, by the Usher of the Black Rod, or his authorized Deputy; and every Witness is allowed his reasonable expenses, to be taxed by The Senate, or any Officer thereof appointed for that purpose.

82. Witnesses refusing to obey the Summons are, by Order of the Senate, taken into the custody of the Usher of the Black Rod, and not liberated therefrom, except by Order of The Senate, and after payment of the expenses incurred.

83. Every Bill of Divorce is to be prepared in the English and French languages by the party applying for the same, and printed by the Con-tractor for the Sessional Printing for The Senate, at the expense of the party; and five hundred copies thereof, in English, and two hundred copies in French, must be deposited in the Office of The Clerk of The Senate, and no such Bill is to be read a third time until a certificate from the Queen's Printer shall have been filed with The Clerk, that the cost of printing 500 copies of the Act in English, and 250 copies in French for the Government, has been paid to him.

84. Every applicant for a Bill of Divorce, at the time of presenting the Petition, is to pay into the hands of The Clerk of The Senate, a sum of One hundred dollars, to cover the expenses which may be incurred by the Senate during the progress of the Bill.

85. In all unprovided cases, reference should be had to the Rules and Decisions of the House of Lords.

APPENDIX III.

FORM OF PETITION TO THE THREE BRANCHES OF THE LEGISLATURE, FOR A PRIVATE BILL.

Form of
Petition to
His Excel-
lency.

To His Excellency the Right Honorable Sir
JOHN YOUNG, Baronet, K.C.G., G.C.M.G.,
Governor General of Canada, &c., &c., &c.,*

IN COUNCIL.

The Petition of the undersigned   of the
    of

HUMBLY SHEWETH:

        That (*here state the object de-sired by the petitioner in soliciting an Act*).

Wherefore your petitioner humbly prays that
Your Excellency may be pleased to sanction
the passing of an Act (*for the purposes above
mentioned*).

And as in duty bound, your petitioner will ever
pray.

        (Signature) { Seal, in the case
       of an existing
      Corporation.

(*Date.*)

---

* Petitions to the Lieut. Governor of Quebec, are addressed,
"To His Honor Sir NARCISSE FORTUNAT BELLEAU, Knight,
Lieutenant Governor of the Province of Quebec."

(*To either House.*)

* To the Honorable the $\left\{\begin{array}{l}\text{Senate}\\\text{House of Commons}\end{array}\right\}$
of Canada, in Parliament assembled :

The Petition of the undersigned   of the
   of

HUMBLY SHEWETH :

   That (*here state the object desired by the petitioner in soliciting an Act.*)

  Wherefore your petitioner humbly prays that
  Your Honorable House may be pleased
  to pass an Act (*for the purposes above mentioned*).

  And as in duty bound, your petitioner will
  ever pray.

    (Signature) $\{$ Seal, as above.

(*Date.*)

---

 * Petitions to the Legislature of Quebec are addressed,
"To the Honorable the $\left\{\begin{array}{l}\text{Legislative Council}\\\text{Legislative Assembly}\end{array}\right\}$ of the Province
of Quebec, in Provincial Parliament assembled."

INDEX.

13

Officers of the House :

May not act as Parliamentary agents, 31.

Opposition to private bills :

Unusual at second reading, except on general principles, or on the ground of interference with public rights, 98.

Before select committee, 72.

Petitions against a bill, stand referred to committee thereon, 56, 127.

Arrangement between the parties for selection of a day for considering an opposed bill, 71.

Opponents should present a petition, specifying grounds of objection, 73.— Limited to the grounds so stated, *ib.*—May be heard by counsel, 74.

Opposition held to be abandoned, if no parties appear when petition is read, 73.

Locus standi of opponents, 77.

Opposition to clauses, 78.

Parties having diverse interests may not avail themselves, on their own account, of a notice issued by other parties, 52 ;—but if a bill be abandoned by its promoters, the committee may permit other parties to proceed with it, 94.

Orders of the Day :

Place assigned to private bills on the Orders of each day in the week, 100.

Parliamentary Agents :

Employment of, in Commons, 29, 132.

Cannot act without the authority of the Speaker. 30, 133.

Mode of qualifying, 30.

Members and officers of the House disqualified from acting, 30.

Registered, 31.

Subject to a prohibition to practise, for any violation of the Rules or practice of Parliament, 30, 133.

Patents of Invention :

Placed under control of the Parliament of Canada, 13.

Petitions :

Every private bill to be based on a petition, 32. (Form in Appendix III.) —Certain bills rejected, not being founded on petitions, 10, 33.

Not to be signed by agents, but by the parties themselves, 32.

Mode of presentation to each branch of the Legislature, 32.

Railways—continued.

Standing Committee on Railways, Canals, and Telegraph Lines, appointment of, 64.

All bills relating to Railways, &c., referred, 56.

Instructions to, 66.

Powers and duties of the committee are similar to those of the Private Bill Committee,—See *Private Bill Committee.*

Rates or Tolls :

Bills involving the same ought to be first brought into the Commons, 4.

Amount thereof to be printed in the bill in *italics*, to be filled up by committee, 55, 87.

Practice of Imperial Parliament in regard to imposition of a local rate, 89, (and Note.)

Re-commitment :

Bills may be re-committed, after report of committee of whole, 108 ;—before third reading, 109.—To the select committee, 95.

Reports of committees on private bills :

That preamble is not proved, 80.

That alterations have been made in the preamble, 85.

Recommending an extension of provisions of bill, 92.

Calling attention to unusual provisions, or such as exceed the limits of the notice,—or amendments of a peculiar nature, 87, 129.

That certain bills referred are public rather than private in their character, 8.

Every bill referred must be reported, 94, 129.

Evidence not usually reported, except by special order, 95.

Time for receiving reports limited, 96, 122.

Representation :

Local bills affecting the Representation, treated as public bills, 9.

Royal Assent :

Given to private bills in the same manner as public bills, 119.

Rules relative to private bills :

Notice to be given of a motion to suspend any Rule, 110, 131.

No motion for suspending 51st Rule (Notices) to be made until after report of Committee on Standing Orders, 47, 126.—Motion made, when required, after report, and before presentation of bill, 54.

Published in Official Gazette, and the substance in other papers, 123.

FINIS.

www.ingramcontent.com/pod-product-compliance
Lightning Source LLC
Chambersburg PA
CBHW020545270326
41927CB00006B/730